Advance Praise
The Clarity Con...

"As President and CEO of a large and diverse region like Latin America, my biggest challenge is keeping teams across different countries **focused and motivated on top priorities and strategy execution regardless of their day-to-day** distractions and difficulties. This book provides a clearer, better, and simpler way to improve our decision-making process. With the Clarity Compass, Dr. Brit Poulson has developed **a powerful and simple tool** for leading a group of high-performance individuals from different areas by helping to deal with daily challenges in a much more effective manner and building stronger team relationships. I strongly recommend it to current and future business leaders looking for impactful management tools."

—Jose Luis Valls, President and CEO of Nissan Latin America

"Making lasting change in your life or career takes courage and requires overcoming a natural fear of something new. Dr. Poulson's Clarity Compass is **an ideal framework for becoming a more effective leader and enjoying life** on your terms."

—David Meerman Scott, bestselling author of *The New Rules of Marketing & PR*

*"As a coach, I've used different techniques to effect personal transformation, like aligning intentions with actions, finding limiting beliefs, and writing life stories. **The Clarity Compass is a simple and easy method that does it all.** Better yet, Brit Poulson explains his method in an easy-to-read and engaging manner. The resulting book just might be a life-changer for its readers."*

—Karen Phelan, Cofounder of Operating Principals and author of the bestselling *I'm Sorry I Broke Your Company*

*"Cash is not king. **In a world so filled with doubt and mistrust, clarity is king.** You will find no better guide to learning it, coming from it and teaching it to others than the guidance, wisdom and clarity you will discover in the Clarity Compass."*

—Dr. Mark Goulston, author of *Just Listen: Discover the Secret to Getting Through to Absolutely Anyone*

*"The Clarity Compass is a simple learning tool that points the way towards greater effectiveness in our lives and work. Both practical and remarkable, **the principles at the heart of the compass take empowerment to a new level.** For anyone who aspires to greater wellbeing and fulfillment, this is essential for your tool kit!"*

—Fran Fisher, Founding Member, International Coaching Federation

*"Having used the Clarity Compass over the last five years, I believe it is **the most powerful tool on the market** to analyze and navigate complex situations and personal conflicts, at work and at home! It helped me to understand where other people were coming from and to develop strategies for the best ways to approach and deal with highly emotional situations."*

—Tjaard Zwaagstra, VP of Procurement Engineering, Philips Healthcare

*"In these turbulent times, it's increasingly easy to lose our sense of direction in search of some external beacon to show us the way to success—the 'lighthouse' that will lead us 'home.' With his Clarity Compass, Poulson reminds us of the personal way-finder within each of us. Much like an adventure guide, he shows us how to effectively use our internal compass to navigate our 'blind spots.' **This is a worthy resource** for one who wants to take more personal charge of their response to these increasingly complex times."*

—Dan Leahy, Former President of LIOS (Leadership Institute of Seattle)

*"Like a trusted sherpa on a mountain ascension, Dr. Poulson's Clarity Compass will guide you to **reach your potential, shape your future**, and discover your sacred self. Take the first step...."*

—Eric Middleton PhD, University of Michigan Medical School

"The Clarity Compass offers an accessible, yet potent approach to adeptly steer yourself towards your deepest desires and well-being. **Dr. Brit Poulson weaves such heart, depth, and nuance** into a very grounded, strategic path to disentangle from the patterns that hold you back from greater fulfillment in work and life. Putting this book's wisdom into practice will most certainly catalyze your journey!"

—Dr. Deborah Zucker, author of *The Vitality Map*

"To navigate success in a start-up, a corporation, or simply a relationship, one needs not only a continuous reality check but relevant coaching and tools. Rarely can you find all of these in one place, but Dr. Brit Poulson has achieved this with The Clarity Compass. **Buckle up and get ready to be challenged** on how you think you show up compared to how others experience you showing up and use Poulson's method as the way to drive congruence between the two. Once this is achieved, your true north will be discovered and the new 'you' will be unleashed!"

—Christopher Smith, National Strategy Practice Lead at Grant Thornton, LLP

"My mentor, the great Peter Drucker, said that our mission in life should be to make a positive difference, not to prove how smart or right we are. The Clarity Compass builds effectively on this premise, showing us how to let go of ego, see past blind spots and sharpen our under-standing of the world around us. **Well worth reading!**"

—Marshall Goldsmith, executive coach and author of *Triggers*

"This powerful book illuminates the simple truth that clarity of direction is not about having all of the right an-swers, but rather about asking all of the right questions. Poulson does **a masterful job** of guiding you through a process to gain insights that enable you to live with in-tention and integrity."

—Lois P. Frankel, PhD, author of *Nice Girls Don't Get the Corner Office*

"As the Chief Executive of several large manufacturing companies, I almost always found the most challenging issues were people issues. The Clarity Compass offers a unique and valuable set of concepts that help untangle the complexities involved and move on to effective solu-tions. The pairing of Intentions/Actions and Facts/Stories is a key point. The Clarity Compass will become **a must read for all aspiring leaders** and for individuals seeking insights into their own behavior."

—Henry Schacht, Former CEO of Cummins and Lucent; Board of Yale, Chase, Johnson & Johnson, and CBS

"All too often, we are our own worst enemy in our ef-forts to change. The Clarity Compass was designed to help us break through our resistance, illuminate our blind spots, and improve our decision-making. Dr. Brit Poulson has **provided an ingenious tool that is provocative and challenging**. Not only can it change beliefs, it can transform lives. The Clarity Compass can assist its users to lead happier, more fulfilling lives."

—Stanley Krippner, PhD, Professor of Psychology, Saybrook University and co-author of *Personal Mythology*

The Clarity Compass

SEE MORE CLEARLY.

HAVE CREATIVE CONVERSATIONS.

LIVE THE LIFE YOU WANT.

Dr. Brit Poulson

VISION CREATION PUBLISHING

SEATTLE, WASHINGTON

Dr. Brit Poulson/Vision Creation Publishing
2545 NE 95th ST
Seattle, WA 98115
www.clarity-compass.com

Cover Design: Thomas DeHart

Ordering Information:
Quantity sales. Special discounts are available on quantity purchases by corporations, associations, and others. For details, contact the "Special Sales Department" at the address above.

The Clarity Compass/ Dr. Brit Poulson —1st ed.
ISBN 978-0-9707328-1-1

*'It ain't what you don't know that gets you in trouble.
It's what you know for sure that just ain't so.'*

—A QUOTE SOME EXPERTS IRONICALLY KNOW FOR SURE
WAS SAID BY MARK TWAIN, BUT OTHERS BELIEVE IT
AIN'T SO

Contents

Part Two: The Clarity Compass for Other

Acknowledgements

I want to acknowledge the following authors, whose books influenced me personally and prompted me to create a more accessible format of this book: Stephen Covey – *Seven Habits of Highly Effective People*, Og Mandino - all of his inspirational books, Dale Carnegie – *How to Win Friends and Influence People*, and Zander and Zander – *The Art of Possibility*. *The Clarity Compass* originally grew out of the most basic of traditional communication models (my intention – my filter – modality – other's filter – impact on other) and eventually merged with psychological constructs, such as cognitive psychology, Carl Jung's version of psychodynamics, and Martin Heidegger's writings on hermeneutic philosophy.

I want to thank Gary Dallas, Joel Pitney, and Erin Merrihew for the significant contribution that each made in the development, writing, and editing of this book. There are a number of other folks that directly contributed to this book with their thinking, feedback, and moral support whom I would also like to name: Miranda Poulson (my daughter), Britt & Joannie Poulson (my father and late mother), Greg Flynn, Nessie White, Brian Arbanas, Jack Richbourg, Dan Leahy, Donald Williamson, Meghann McNiff, Lismary de Lemos, Tom Skillman, Tjaard Zwaagstra, Luca Dellacroce, and Eric Middleton.

Invitation

"I hate the Clarity Compass."

He went by the name of Deck: He was ex-military, business casual, with pictures of his kids and Chihuahuas meticulously placed on his desk. This was my third leadership coaching session with him. He stretched out in his chair, his designer loafers crossed on the hardwood floor between us and his gaze landing on the conference room ceiling.

"Why's that?" I asked.

He shifted to look me in the eye. "I love being right. And the Clarity Compass shows me that I'm not."

We all like to be right.

One of the hallmarks of strong leadership is having confidence in your decisions. Strong leadership entails displaying enough certainty to motivate a friend, inspire a team, or lead a company. How do you maintain that confidence if you let doubt poison your conviction, or even worse, if you have to admit you were wrong?

The utilization of a compass implies having a clear direction towards an outcome. And, ironically, in my work I've found that it's only in learning to "soften" your own perspective on what is right that you can discover, define, and practice the best directions, outcomes, and actions. So while being right may be gratifying, we both know that blindly charging ahead and relying only on your sense of certainty will leave you lost and alone. Unfounded certainty starts with your Ego, whose job is to reduce pain and increase control, comfort, and safety. Yet by being over controlling, it frequently gets in your way, and sometimes trips you up completely. That's where the Clarity Compass comes in.

The Clarity Compass is a tool designed to support you in being more effective and skillful in terms of helping you get out of your own way and to where you want to be—with greater speed, grace, and ease.

Sure, Deck—like a lot of people—hated the Clarity Compass at first. It made him uncomfortable. However, he continues to use it because it helps him to set aside his love of being right for the sake of being productive. It invites him to shed everything unfounded about the way he has viewed his work. It provides him with a clearer perspective, and the means to act on it. Three years later, Deck's biotech company has almost doubled in size. Among his clients and employees, his reputation is at an all-time high. His professional relationships have never been better.

Given the significant transformation I've seen with hundreds of people like Deck, I want to ask you a question: While in many situations you *could* be both right and effective, if it came down to a choice... which would you rather be?

Preface

Most people, even those who rate themselves as "highly satisfied" with their relationships, finances, and general wellbeing, want to improve their lives. It's an inborn human impulse to strain against "good" in the pursuit of "better." You likely picked up this book because you recognize this impulse in yourself and are seeking a new tool with which to improve your circumstances, your efficiency, or perhaps your relationships—professional and personal.

You have already come to terms with the idea that what you have tried in the past hasn't worked, and might not have been right for you. This humility shows a fundamental hope, that in the future, there may be better answers and solutions to the questions you are facing.

The Clarity Compass is a tool that can guide you to greater effectiveness, improve your relationships, and, ultimately, transform your life.

Comprised of the Two Polarities, Intentions to Actions and Facts vs. Stories, the Four Directions of the Clarity Compass will challenge you to look both inside yourself and out to the world around you, providing the insights to achieve new levels of success.

In working with leadership and transformation since 1983, I've seen the positive impact the Clarity Compass has had on people. I am not suggesting that I definitely have all of the answers. Everyone's path is different, but I will say that the Clarity Compass has worked well for my leadership consulting clients and for me personally. I've seen individuals blossom from reserved wallflowers into go-getters, and from bullies into the kind of people you'd want to work beside. I've seen successful people *thrive beyond what they ever thought possible*, and I believe the Clarity Compass can do the same for you.

Reality Maps & Blind Spots

Before "picking up" and using the Clarity Compass, it is crucial that we begin to understand the ways in which we are not seeing the world clearly, and the negative impact this has on our lives. In my experience, I have seen that despite hard work and diligence, people are consistently ineffective or completely blocked because of the Blind Spots in their Reality Maps.

What are Reality Maps and Blind Spots?

Reality Maps are blueprints that reflect the way we have thought about and constructed our lives; they also inform the way we continue to think about and build our worldview.

Blind Spots are inaccuracies in our Reality Maps. When explored and discovered, they reveal differences between how we see the world and how the world actually is. Blind Spots are areas where we don't know what ⁀don't know. They tend to create challenges in how ⁀ld, especially in how we relate to

y using the Clarity Compass, we y Maps, spread them out before making them as accurate and as ssible.

s helps us turn our unconscious ns into conscious decisions and f my clients, Sean, to illustrate this ral inclination for being a states- ayor and was known for his calm ughtful and precise statements. rally to Sean. Although his easy was reassuring, some people saw s too close to his chest. This was a was seen as honest, but not forth- perspectives and opinions, which stworthy to some people.

ot see how this was impacting his through his first Clarity Compass e to see his Blind Spot and how it He has since worked diligently to y in his conversations and relation- d him to build better trust with his ⁀.

, of course, at play in our person-

---

to all and general in its nature is not as binding as one that is entirely personal and specific; that if others do not do their part, our share of the blame is comparatively small; that where the difficulties are very great, obedience cannot be an absolute demand; that if we are willing to do our best, this is all that can be asked of us.

Christians, this is not obedience! This is not the spirit in which the first disciples accepted it. This is not the spirit in which we wish to live with our beloved Lord. We want to say—each one of us—if there be no one else, "I, by His grace, will give myself and my life to live for His kingdom." Let me for a moment separate myself from all others and think of my personal relation to Jesus.

I am a member of Christ's body. He expects every member to be at His disposal, to be animated by His Spirit, to live for what He is and does. It is so with my physical body. I carry every member with me day by day in the assurance that I can count on each one to do its part. Our Lord has taken me so truly up into His body that He can ask and expect nothing else from me. And I have so truly yielded myself to Him that there can be no idea of my wanting anything but just to know and do His will.

Or let me take the illustration of the vine and the branches. The branch has just as much only one object for its being as the vine—bearing fruit. If I really am a branch, I am just as much as He was in the world—only and wholly to bring forth fruit, to live and labor for the salvation of men.

Take still another illustration. Christ has bought me with His blood. No slave conquered by force or purchased al lives. Take my friends, Bill and Jasmine, for example. They're a married couple who have struggled with their daughter's substance abuse issues. Trying to deal with the fact that their daughter has been in and out of rehab has caused an increasing amount of tension and distance in their relationship. This tension first manifested itself in one of our Clarity Compass sessions, when Jasmine made an offhanded comment. She told Bill, "You care more about your work than our daughter." Bill was shocked and hurt. Fortunately, prior to this particular session, both Bill and Jasmine had developed enough skills to talk through the situation by exploring their Blind Spots.

Bill's Blind Spot revolved around the fact that he had seen himself as the main family provider. He was focused on making sure they could afford rehab in addition to comfortably managing their usual yearly expenses. But more importantly, in this specific situation he saw himself as needing to be strong for his wife and daughter. This prompted him to keep his anxiety and fears to himself. Jasmine had interpreted his lack of *expressed* concern as not being concerned at all. Even worse, she thought he considered their daughter as "just another project."

The Blind Spots in Bill's Reality Maps centered around being stoic and strong, and not realizing his wife's need to connect with him about concerns over their daughter. Jasmine's Blind Spots stemmed from not understanding what Bill's concerns looked like, and not expressing her own sadness about her husband's lack of expression.

These two sets of Blind Spots fed off of one another, creating more distance and resentment, until Jasmine erupted and took that verbal jab at Bill. Fortunately, the couple was able to use Jasmine's comment to break the

HE LAST COMMAND

ifising love. It lies in the very
t every member of His body, in
Him, feels himself urged to
ved. The command is no arbi-
is simply the revelation for our
consent of the wonderful truth
t we now occupy His place on
d love now carry out through us
hat now in His stead we live to
winning a lost world back to

has failed in obeying the com-
ians there are who never knew
mmand! Many hear of it but do
ves to obey it! And many seek to
measure as seem to them fitting

g what obedience is. We have
ves up to a wholehearted obedi-
ared to gladly listen to anything
lerstand and carry out this our
command: the Gospel to every

t I have to say under the three
t His command. Place yourself
. Begin at once to live for His

His Command
gs that weaken the force of this
command. There is the impression that a command given

89

ice, letting them explore and reveal their Blind Spots. Using the Clarity Compass, they were able to come back together again into a partnership that effectively and warmly supported their daughter.

For my clients, every challenge that arises is rooted in the Blind Spots inherent in their Reality Maps. In every case, when my clients examine the accuracy of their Reality Maps and uncover their Blind Spots, profound change begins to occur. Things begin to shift. Obstacles fall away. Creative opportunities appear. When you take a thorough look at your life—when you face your Reality Maps and Blind Spots head on—transformation is inevitable. Imagination and creativity awaken. Your life naturally responds.

The Clarity Compass works best when you open yourself up to different ways of seeing things. Examine the areas of your life that scare you the most. Permit yourself to be vulnerable in the pursuit of transformation. This process isn't trivial; it is the Heart of bravery. It takes tremendous courage to scrutinize yourself at this level, and to see yourself as someone who can change and grow.

The "Big Challenge"

To make your experience of this book as pragmatic as possible, I encourage you to select one "Big Challenge" or opportunity to work on while reading. This challenge can stem from your work or family life. Choose a situation that involves another person, one where you are willing to invest time and energy into improving the relationship.

The following might trigger a situation that has been plaguing you. Are the Monday morning meetings Joe leads unproductive? Is your teenager leaving a mess in the living room or kitchen? Is Ben, the head of your marketing team, bickering with your sales team? Are you personally overwhelmed by the number of emails that you are receiving from Susan? Are you and your husband having trouble communicating about money?

Applying the Clarity Compass to your "Big Challenge" as you read will deepen your understanding of the problem-solving tools I present, and will begin to move your situation toward improved outcomes.

In the first half of the book, you will learn to use the Clarity Compass from your own perspective—that is, for the **Self**—to uncover and address any Blind Spots in how you are perceiving a situation. Later, you will learn to use the Clarity Compass to work to ascertain the perspective of someone else—that is, for the **Other**—to uncover and address any Blind Spots in how you perceive them.

Use the Clarity Compass like an adventurer: Explore, navigate, and map the wilderness that is your inner self. Let the Clarity Compass guide you through the conflicts, challenges, and opportunities life throws your way. See these elements of your life not as drudgery to fight through, but as an adventure you can navigate in order to grow, flourish, and experience more joy.

Part One:
The Clarity Compass for Self

Part One:
The Clarity Compass Model

Years ago, my brother came to see me from Florida. He had visited, but never traveled around the majestic Pacific Northwest. So, I planned a road trip from Seattle to Vancouver. From the airport, my brother, daughter, and I headed north on I-5, crossing into Canada well past dinnertime. These were the days before smartphones and GPS.

"Where's the hotel?" My brother asked.

"I didn't book one," I said. "I figured we could just drive around and find one."

For reasons that now escape me, this had seemed like a sensible plan. As it turned out, however, finding a hotel in Vancouver on a Friday night during rush-hour traffic was no simple task. With my brother and daughter becoming increasingly frustrated—picture not only your child asking "How much longer?" from the back seat, but the sibling you're trying to host clenching his growling stomach—I surrendered control. I did what most men hate to do: I pulled the car over so we could call my brother's wife in Florida and ask her find us a place to stay online.

Here's the lesson: Before setting out on a trip, you

need to know where you're going and how to get there. You need a compass.

The Two Polarities

In this chapter, I will be introducing the Clarity Compass model in broad strokes to give you a general sense of the terrain before exploring it in more detail later. As stated in the introduction, the purpose of the Clarity Compass model is to help you better uncover your Blind Spots. This allows you to better navigate your Reality Maps and become a happier, more effective person!

As you can see in the figure below, the Clarity Compass is organized into Two Polarities that are comprised of Four Directions:

The First Polarity, Intentions to Actions, runs from north to south. Intentions in the Clarity Compass help us explore what we want to create, as well as the mysterious, yet powerful forces that drive our desires. Actions are the creative steps we take toward achieving our goals.

This north-south polarity represents the idea that as

you become aware of and crystallize your Intentions, the Actions you generate will produce more meaningful results.

The Second Polarity, Facts vs. Stories, runs along the east-west horizontal axis. Facts deal with direct observations, as well as what we *choose* to observe. Stories are composed of our beliefs, interpretations, opinions, and emotional responses. This polarity represents the idea that by discerning objective Facts from subjective Stories, you uncover your blocks, or Blind Spots, and imagine new opportunities.

The point of the polarities is *contrast*. With the Intentions to Actions Polarity, we are contrasting envisioning an outcome that meets a need, and then moving from the vision and actualizing it in a powerful way that generates an outcome. With the Facts versus Stories polarity, a contrast is made between what is objectively true and our subjective interpretations. As Facts and Stories are contrasted, the objective Facts become clearer and the Stories can be more deeply investigated.

It is through these contrasting elements of the Clarity Compass that Blind Spots tend to be revealed. Once you begin the work of transformation—opening yourself up to bigger and better possibilities—you begin to trip over the parts of your Reality Maps that aren't quite accurate. Your Blind Spots begin showing up like rocks or tree roots, and you stub your toe. You almost fall. You catch yourself and say, "Ah-ha! I just ran into a Blind Spot!"

As you begin working with the Clarity Compass, you will recognize that you already possess all the tools you need. You just have to polish and hone them before your mind will shift into a new gear. All those moments that felt "off" or uncomfortable at work, at home, or at the tennis club will be revealed in a new light: "I see! I'm not perfect and I'm not always right. I have Blind Spots." It is quite likely that you've always known this, but when you bring a book like this one into your life, you are fully admitting that there is so much more to know and so many different ways to do things. You don't have all the answers. By opening yourself up to new possibilities and ways of thinking, you can set your life on a new trajectory. Congratulations!

Had I used the Clarity Compass *before* my great Pacific Northwest adventure from Seattle to Vancouver, I would have quickly thought through the following (and probably would have heard my daughter and my brother say, "Congratulations on organizing such a great trip!"):

- **What are my Intentions?** Have an easy and fun trip, be a good host to my brother, take care of my daughter, and make sure everyone is having a good time.
- **What are the best Actions?** Think through who I should reach out to: Who might be crucial to having a good trip? Consider restaurant and motel staff, and friends who are familiar with the area.
- **What are the Facts?** I scheduled to go to a different country with my brother and daughter, on a weekend, where we would be arriving in Friday afternoon traffic with no accommodations lined up.
- **What Story am I telling myself?** Because Vancouver B.C. is a big city with many options, we will be able to pull up to motel, walk in, and get a room.

If I had taken just a few minutes to walk through these steps, I would have increased my awareness of what I was getting into and what inaccurate Stories I was making up. In finding and naming my Blind Spots, I would've planned better.

The intention of this book is to support you in understanding the Clarity Compass well enough to apply it to immediate or future situations. You may simply want to make your next weekend getaway with your spouse amazing, or you may be in charge of merging two major divisions of your Fortune 500 Corporation. No matter the size or impact of the challenge, using the Clarity Compass can significantly improve the results you achieve or the effects your Actions have on others.

CHAPTER 2

Reality Maps

We briefly examined Reality Maps during the preface, and now it's time to explore this foundational concept more deeply. Each of us relies on our unique Reality Maps in order to make sense of the world. We begin building these maps when we are young, and we rely on them to help us navigate the world and make good decisions. I use the plural "Maps" because I believe that, just as there are many versions of physical maps, like countries, states, and towns, we also hold many Reality Maps. And just as local maps are congruent with larger, regional maps, our brain tries to create as much congruency as possible between maps for specific situations and maps for larger worldviews. Said another way: Our smaller maps tend to give more detail than our broader maps when it comes to "reading" specific people or situations.

There is nothing inherently wrong with having Reality Maps. In fact, they are necessary because they allow us to mark our way, track our progress, and function in the world. But problems arise when we mistake our maps for the territory.

You see, it is human nature to assume that our Reality Maps are true and accurate, and we constantly mistake them for reality itself. The Blind Spots they contain can function like tinted glasses we have forgotten we are wearing, until we need to take them off. Sure, those tinted lenses make everything look pretty and guard our eyes—but sometimes, in order to grow or make a long overdue change, we need to do the exact opposite of what our eye doctors told us. Once in a while, when we know something "isn't quite working," we have to take off those shades and stare directly into the glare. Seeing the world more directly won't blind us. It will illuminate what we have been avoiding or missing. Our willingness to open our eyes and see directly what is there will "heal" our Blind Spots!

Reality Maps are not passive repositories of information, but rather they are active processing centers of new, continuously incoming information. As we receive new data, it is filtered into our Reality Maps based on what's already there—Blind Spots and all.

In many ways, Reality Maps provide a blueprint of life based on our experience. They are cognitive structures that not only reflect what we think, but also represent everything about our perceived reality. They encompass our experience of the physical realm, our visceral or emotional expectations, and our values.

Our Reality Maps allow us to move through the world believing we are "right" or "mostly right." Blind Spots are the places where our mental models break down without our conscious realization. They are areas in which our personal Reality Maps differ from actual reality. Don't beat yourself up for having Blind Spots—we all have them, and most result from the unavoidable limits of the human perspective.

My Reality Maps, for example, included a belief that if I hired and paid someone for services, they would simply deliver those services. But repeatedly, I was paying people and they were not delivering what they had promised. What was my role in this? How was I creating and then "tripping over" this obstacle in my Reality Maps? Investigating these questions, I discovered that I had neglected to create contracts that spelled out the specific terms of our arrangements. This left room for discrepancy between what I expected of my employees or contract professionals, and what they felt they were being paid to do. This was a significant Blind Spot on my part, but it was probably as obvious to you as the need to book a hotel ahead of time for a weekend in Vancouver.

Note too, that while I have gotten better at creating contracts more frequently and accurately, there are times when I still don't think a contract is necessary. Even in these new and improved contracts I create, I often don't think to add particular nuances that end up being significant. I am sharing where I struggle because I find that this is true for most people: In areas where we have significant Blind Spots, we typically work hard to cut the distance between where we are and where we want to be in half. We repeat this process—we hone in on that distance and continually try to reduce it. And while we work hard to cut the distance in half, we never fully reach the other end.

To get an idea of how starkly different Reality Maps can be, think about politics and politicians. Think of the most recent or upcoming national election. Think of all of those people who support the candidate or policies you are against. How is it that so many people support a person and policies that seem so absolutely untenable to you? Who *are* these people and how can so many of them be so off base? Now recognize that these people ask the very same questions of you and your candidate.

As you work with Reality Maps and Blind Spots, recognize that there are billions of people on the planet, and each can only see through their perspective. *You* can only see through your perspective, and your Reality Maps are incomplete. They cannot reflect the entirety of the world as it actually is. Recognize that there will always be another way to see things—that your experience of the world is inherently subjective—and you will have taken the first step towards radical clarity.

One note of caution: Please be patient with yourself as you awaken to your Blind Spots and work to improve your thinking and behavior. I have found that expecting too much from yourself only increases denial and actually strengthens Blind Spots.

Blind Spots

It makes sense that we humans have Blind Spots because we do *not* have an infinite capacity to process an infinite universe, and there are ways we each have limited perspectives. Think of a periscope, rising through the ocean waves and allowing the submarine captain below a view of what lies above the surface. The captain understands that his vision is limited to what the periscope can see. There is no peripheral vision. There is only this single, limited perspective.

Each of us peers out from our inner world in a similar way. So much of what we think about the world is based on the limited information we receive when we put our periscopes "up" and look through them. And all too often, instead of receiving and processing information in an intelligent fashion, we simply use the new data to confirm what we already believe.

The Clarity Compass will enable you to operate your periscope more effectively by broadening your view of life and giving you tools to not only better evaluate the information you receive, but to also act more efficiently and wisely upon it.

The 3 Types of Blind Spots

There are endless ways in which our Reality Maps do not match up with reality. As we examine our own perspective for Blind Spots, let's break them up into three primary categories:

1. **We are wrong.** In these cases, our *understanding* of reality and reality itself just don't match. This can be as simple as remembering the wrong name of a capital city or a financial number. It could also be something as broad as completely misperceiving how a financial system works or a country's location on the map. We can be wrong in our assumptions about interpersonal situations, like when we don't hear someone correctly and draw incorrect conclusions as a result.

2. **We have biases.** We understand something well enough, but there's a slight bend to how we are representing ourselves or the information we have. This leads us to make decisions that are slightly off. When we stereotype, for example, we incorrectly label another culture's values. Or, we may respect authority figures, but defer to them in a way that does a disservice to both them and ourselves. Or,

we believe that we need to take care of ourselves. But if we don't sometimes rely on others or know how to ask for help, we become overburdened and don't give other people a chance to support us.

3. **We are missing information.** Here, it's not that we are wrong, but there is simply something missing in terms of data, a concept, or an experience. We think we understand our taxes well, but we miss out on a big deduction because we were unaware of it. Or, we work on a project all night only to find out that someone else had completed it the day before.

I find it helpful to divide Blind Spots into these three categories because it helps us to more quickly recognize them in ourselves. I encourage you to take a moment to think of some Blind Spots you observe in others (since it is hard to access our own), and then break them out into each of the categories above.

Of course, saying, "I was wrong; I have biases; I am missing information," isn't easy, nor is accepting the subjective nature of your perspective. If we aren't actively utilizing a tool as powerful as the Clarity Compass, we only tend to discover our Blind Spots when we encounter a personal struggle or come face-to-face with people whose Reality Maps don't match up with our own.

Disagreement, particularly over the things we've held to be true, can be unpleasant. It can make us angry and confused, or even sad and afraid. These emotions often render us defensive, and spur us unconsciously to try even harder to convince others that our Reality Maps are definitely right and infallible. These feelings could signal that we are avoiding a conflict that might show us we are wrong. Pay attention to these signals—they indicate that your Ego is trying to take control!

The Ego and the Heart

The Ego has the enormously complex and crucial job of helping maintain your safety and comfort. It does whatever it can to help you survive and remain stable. It supports your pleasure, and urges you to avoid pain and chaos. The Ego is not the problem, but problems do arise if the Ego is left unchecked. Because we rely on the Ego so heavily, we tend to let it take over. When we do, the Ego can develop into an all-powerful despot, championing the Reality Maps it has created over the years and insisting, "Yes! This is right. This is the only right way. You can count on this."

At worst, the Ego squirms and reacts at the first hint of ambiguity, and avoids being wrong at all costs. It declares your Reality Maps to be the ultimate truth, and convinces you there are no Blind Spots. At the very least, it assures you that a piece of information you're receiving in a particular moment is false, and not a Blind Spot.

One of the Ego's primary functions is to avoid the feeling of "cognitive dissonance," which occurs when we believe two incongruent things at the same time. Cognitive dissonance makes us feel "mentally uncomfortable." Since the Ego likes to keep us in our comfort zone, it works diligently to reconcile conflicting beliefs, or to numb the feelings of dissonance. This can lead to a number of cognitive biases, especially confirmation bias, where we actively engage in pursuing data that proves what we already know or believe.

For example, I believe that I am especially plagued with technical issues. It seems I buy devices that are advertised as the fastest and strongest, but then they somehow work at a glacial speed. Or, the programs I use frequently stop working for no apparent reason, while everybody else seems to zip along. No matter what, I keep my tech person busy. Even though I know it's crazy to believe that somehow technology is singling me out and thwarting my best intentions, part of me still believes it.

I'm not proud to share with you the fact that this tech "paranoia" is part of my Reality Maps, but I'm hoping you receive this confession as part of my conviction that we all have crazy, or even false, patches in our Reality Maps. Our Egos are very attached to believing XYZ, even if a more rational part of our mind says that XYZ is crazy. This is the Ego operating largely from confirmation bias. So every time something goes wrong with the technology I'm using, I say, "See! Can you believe I have this many problems with technology? Technology and I are not friends!"

Of course, technology frustrates most people from time to time, but focusing on my particularly bad relationship with technology makes me miserable. Yet, even though I know this perspective makes me miserable, at least it confirms my Reality Maps. My Ego says, "Yes, I am happy. This reinforces the internal belief about technology, which I, the Ego, hold to be consistently true." Bias confirmed.

You can see why it is hard to confront the Ego with the truth. It's hard to acknowledge our own subjective biases, and harder still to move into new territory beyond what we already know that threatens our sense of security. So most of us just carry on, using the Reality Maps our Ego has helped construct, pretending our Blind Spots don't matter or exist. We use unfounded confidence to propel us through the day or toward a goal, often at the expense of taking Actions that would otherwise have ensured positive outcomes—as I did when we set out on that road trip to Canada. This false sense of security often perpetuates an underlying insecurity and creates areas of continually poor results. These results can then urge the Ego toward even more desperate ways of proving its sense of competence.

But it doesn't have to be this way. If we can learn to manage the Ego's need to be right/better/in power, we can free it to serve our overall wellbeing. To do so requires Heart.

Where Ego represents control, safety, comfort, and cognitive consistency, Heart represents almost the direct opposite. Heart is for imagination, courage, and connection (to ourselves, others, and the world). Where Ego says, "Stick to what you know," Heart says, "Let's have an adventure."

For example, in writing this book, my Ego has nudged me to quit numerous times. As my Ego examined the expenditure of time, money, focus, and energy—let alone the impact on other areas of my life—it would try to convince me: "It's not worth it. You really don't know what difference this book is going to make to the lives of others, or to yours. You're not a writer anyway. You're a leadership consultant and executive coach. Stick to what you know."

But my Heart tells me a different story. While my Heart is highly grateful for my time with clients, it is yearning for the opportunity to bring the Clarity Compass to more people in the world. It is thrilling to think of more people being motivated to operate creatively, openly, and compassionately, and to thus make a greater contribution at home, work, and to the community at large. Our hearts exclaim, "Say yes to the possibility of showing up in the world in a new and exciting way, and to engaging with others in a way that's different than what you know. Sure you will continue to make many mistakes and encounter much adversity in this unknown territory, but that's what makes it an adventure!"

You can see the difference in perspective between the Heart and the Ego. We must use our Hearts to commit ourselves to embracing ambiguity, and *gently and courageously* exploring our Blind Spots. This is a simple, yet radical step toward getting real. Taking this step humbles us the way looking up at a starry sky and contemplating the vastness of the unknown humbles us. By working with the Heart and accepting the incomprehensible and the inherently ambiguous, we free ourselves to seek new perspectives. Then, unbound by our Ego's limits, we learn to take responsibility for the things that are within our healthy control. We can begin to better manage some of the ways we think, and the things we've previously overlooked, misinterpreted, or missed out on because of our Blind Spots. The Clarity Compass invites us to work with the Heart to accept the unknown, and, in doing so, work more effectively with what we *do* know.

Looking back on that trip with my family I could have accepted that I didn't actually know what awaited us in Vancouver. I knew that it was a big city, and I assumed that a hotel would be easily found. Had I accepted that I was driving my family into "uncharted territory," I could have acted in a way that cut down the unknowns. I could have called ahead, determined what things we might want to look at, and—most importantly —made reservations. While the added stress in this family journey was certainly not life-threatening or life-altering, it playfully illustrates where I had Blind Spots, and how because of those Blind Spots, I led us into the wilderness.

As difficult as learning to take responsibility for your life and accepting the unknown can be, you'll find that gently exploring each of the Four Directions spurs creativity and imagination. As William Blake said, "A wise person has a pattern or design in their mind into which everything they know fits and into which everything they don't know could fit."

Blake's quote illustrates the importance of having Reality Maps that are flexible enough to incorporate new information and new perspectives more easily than those that are rigid. As we use the Clarity Compass, not all of our biases and Blind Spots will disappear entirely. Some will merely shrink and others may move in to replace those we get rid of. But once imagination rushes in, it can bridge gaps and build entirely new sections of our Reality Maps, ultimately clearing the path for us to pursue our deepest dreams.

Diamonds and Pearls

We all resist change, and we can all be particularly defensive when it comes to changing our Reality Maps. I've worked with many leaders—talented, thoughtful, open individuals—who are profoundly committed to their work, their people, and their own growth. I've watched each of them resist some call to change. Sensitive people shy away from boldness, and bold people balk at acknowledging their sensitivity. People will deny or defend their traits and behaviors, unwittingly squandering opportunities to grow.

Why is this?

Remember the Ego's commitment to maximizing control and pleasure and minimizing hardship and pain?

Some of the most primitive or foundational aspects of our Reality Maps are pulled from our childhood experiences—the joyful as well as the painful. The Ego influences the construction of our Reality Maps in a way that ensures we keep moving toward joy and is especially determined to keep us from re-experiencing old pain.

Often, our rational conscious decisions—as well as our irrational fears and beliefs—are pre-determined by deep-seated, early formed concepts of the world and are guided in ways that we don't necessarily notice as adults. Because these beliefs have been ingrained in us since childhood and have worked all these years to protect us from pain, they are highly defended. We resist changing many beliefs in our Reality Maps, particularly if we feel they are protecting us from danger and discomfort.

Our defensiveness is, in a way, like a pearl. A piece of sand gets embedded in an oyster, and the oyster treats it like a threat, coating the sand in layer after layer of calcium carbonate, the very substance of the oyster's own shell. What starts off as traumatic is defended against in such a way that something beautiful is created. The defenses against our early pains have become familiar, safe, and sometimes even beautiful to us. We protect our defenses—we clutch at them—as if they were pearls. As a psychology colleague of mine used to say, "We think our s--t is gold."

Many of our pearls *do* serve to keep us safe. For example, we have always been advised against talking to strangers or walking down dark alleys. Or, we learn—often the hard way—not to overcommit to or share personal information with untrustworthy people. But some of our pearls significantly impair our effectiveness and wellbeing. When we guard ourselves to the point of being unfriendly, or stay stuck in a job, relationship, or situation due to an aversion to taking healthy risks, we may be selling ourselves short. If we get in the habit of giving up before following through on important commitments or not sharing ourselves with people we can trust, who knows what opportunities we miss.

Notice that each of my examples illustrates a corollary between the defensive aspects of the pearls that keep us safe versus the defensive aspects of the pearls that impair our effectiveness. This is because we compare the elements of new situations with what we have stored in our Reality Maps. Then we make decisions and act. When the pearls of our Reality Maps are constructed well, we make good decisions and take positive actions to protect ourselves. When our pearls are a bit wonky or maladaptive, we become overly defensive, which does not serve us well.

Diamonds, on the other hand, are formed over eons by intense compression and heat. The atomic structure of carbon is transformed into a crystal, multifaceted and shining. Our *character* is formed like a diamond. It is created by, and subject to, the forces of our environment, making it beautiful and strong. While both the diamond and our character contain imperfections, both are born of powerful and primordial forces. The more we can draw these forces from the buried places within us out into the world, the better.

No matter how dysfunctional the pearls within our Reality Maps may be, we will never rid ourselves of every pearl that is holding a Blind Spot in place. Likewise, we will never unearth every diamond that is lost and buried within our Reality Maps. The best we can do is keep an eye on our Reality Maps, use our Hearts to accept these pearls and diamonds without clinging to them, and begin the hard work of dismantling the aspects of our Reality Maps that don't serve us well. Over time, the Clarity Compass can help you to discern what you want to let go of versus what you want to polish and bring to the world.

Case Studies: The Clarity Compass in Action

To help you understand how the Clarity Compass and its many components can be used to pragmatically support you through day-to-day situations and conversations. I'd like to use the experiences of two of my clients: Deck, the clean-cut, stoic, Clarity Compass-hating, Chihuahua owner whom we met in the introduction; and Matilda, a transplant from Queensland, Australia with a history of competitive open water swimming.

Deck had been the CEO of a high-end biotech firm for nearly five years, and was having problems with employee retention. He couldn't seem to keep any of his immediate staff. He hired qualified people with great track records, paid them well, gave them ample responsibility, and yet they kept leaving the company. In fact, they were dropping like flies. This obviously cut efficiency and resulted in profit and client losses for the company. Deck was mystified.

Matilda, a junior partner at a prominent law firm, wanted to move up into a senior partnership position at her firm. Despite putting in long hours, her performance reviews with her supervisor, Ling, seemed to stall out at mediocre. She was angry and suspicious of her supervisor's motives.

As we move through the following chapters, we'll return to these two clients to see how they used, and benefitted from, the Clarity Compass. We'll track their journeys and explore their discoveries, and at the same time, you'll begin to consider the role the Clarity Compass could play in helping you clear your own path.

You can learn the concepts of the Clarity Compass solely from the experiences of Deck and Matilda, but as you make your way through this book, I encourage you to reflect on your own "Big Challenge" and apply the concepts to it. You might even want to write out how you would respond to your situation after observing how Deck and Matilda apply the Clarity Compass tools.

CHAPTER 3

Intentions to Actions:
The North-South Polarity

As a society, we've become almost frantic with activity. We place more on our plates than we can hold, and we become scattered, fragmented, and overwhelmed. When we are moving about in this state of chaos—which is sometimes subtle and sometimes overwhelming—we lose the time and energy to continue evolving our Reality Maps. In turn, our maps become outdated and inaccurate, and our Blind Spots grow or multiply. Driving clearly and powerfully toward an end result that truly meets our needs often requires great discernment and action that has clear purpose.

The Clarity Compass is a tool we *can* hold onto. If we

can imagine placing our fingers around it in those frantic moments, or when we set out to improve off-kilter situations, we can gain a sense of "true North" and more importantly, we can start to take steps—however many it takes—to get there.

The Flow from Intentions to Actions

The primary idea in the Intentions to Actions polarity is that there is a direct flow between what we are intending and the activity we engage in. If our Intentions are muddled, the Actions that we take will be diffused. As a result, we will feel undermined and frustrated. On the other hand, if we have a crisp and clear purpose, we can drive our activities towards meeting the predominant needs of a given situation.

Our efforts will always be driven by our deeper wants. These deeper wants are translated into outcomes, which we pursue through particular action steps. The more clearly we can articulate our Intentions, the more clarity and focus can flow into the creation and construction of highly leveraged Actions.

Understanding and getting a feel for the deep connection between Intentions and Actions is key to mastering the Clarity Compass. Over the course of this chapter, we'll explore both ends of the polarity in depth. Let's begin with Intentions.

The Intentions Direction

We've spent a lot of time thus far discussing Reality Maps and the Blind Spots we all have when it comes to seeing ourselves, our lives, and our actions more clearly.

The best way to set out on the path to seeing more accurately is to have strong Intentions. The foundation of any endeavor, whether it's to build a better career, home, or relationship, is based on getting clear about our goals. It's critical that we ask ourselves why we do what we do. What do we want to accomplish in the short-term (i.e. in a singular conversation)? Where do we want to land in the long-term (i.e. our hopes for our lives, careers, and relationships)? As we explore our Intentions and begin to consciously choose and cultivate them, we grow our levels of satisfaction and effectiveness.

Lack of clarity in the Intentions direction results in wasted time and wandering about in a malaise you may not even be aware you're in. As you move through the Intentions Direction you will see that the more your outcomes meet specific needs, the more energy you will have. The more aligned those outcomes are to your deeper wants, the better your energy will be utilized. The strongest, most delicious cup of coffee you have ever had might have perked you up, but that jolt of caffeinated confidence is nothing compared to a laser-like focus in the way you orient yourself to the world and specific tasks. Clearly scoped outcomes that meet important needs and deeper wants harness our drive and create greater precision in the efforts we put forth.

So, have that cup of Joe, but then take it to the next level of focus: *What are you trying to make happen?*

The Three Sub-directions of Intentions

For each of the Four Directions of the Clarity Compass, there are three sub-directions that invite us to more deeply understand its particular aspects.

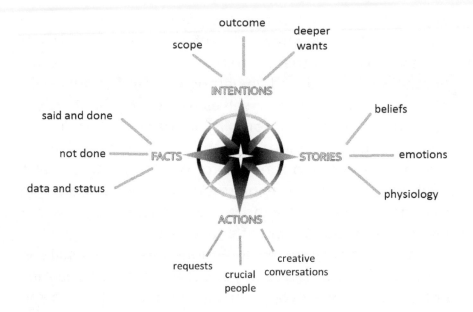

I've had numerous clients get to this point and say, "This is way too complicated. The Clarity Compass requires that I put more time into this situation than I can spare."

I give two responses:

First, for situations where much is at stake, it's worth taking the time to prepare and plan for a better end result. Second, you don't have to follow every single step of the Clarity Compass. At the end of this book, I will introduce a tool called the Speed Compass, which will enable you to use the Clarity Compass without applying all of the different layers and facets of the full version. The Speed Compass is designed to support you quickly. For example, the Speed Compass can be used when you are having a spontaneous conversation or planning a conversation that does not justify the time necessary for going through the entire Clarity Compass.

However, just as your high school English teacher

taught you to master all the English grammar rules before you could break them, using the Speed Compass effectively requires a thorough understanding of each of the Four Directions of the Clarity Compass.

So with that in mind, we will now explore in more depth the three sub directions of Intentions: scope, outcomes, and deeper wants.

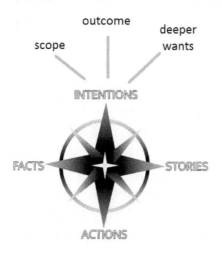

The Intentions direction is about focus, drive, clarity, and energy. We start applying the Clarity Compass process to a given situation by *scoping* the problem and exploring *outcomes*. But ultimately, we're after the *deeper wants* because they provide the "why" energy or drive to move us toward achieving our goals. Once we become clear about our deeper wants, we can revise the scope of our problem and desired outcomes to ensure that we meet them.

One quick reminder: Recall the "Big Challenge" you previously identified and keep it in the back of your mind or make notes for yourself as you read the Intentions Direction, starting with scope.

Scope

For every dream you hold, every situation you explore, and every conflict you face, there is a space between where you are and where you want to be. That space represents the scope of any problem or opportunity. The principle is simple: You cannot address a problem until you fully understand the nature of what you want to change. What is your problem (or opportunity) statement?

My clients usually want to lump several challenges or opportunities into one Clarity Compass exercise, but I advise them not to attempt to tackle all problems at once, or in the same way. Tease out more manageable chunks of the larger situation—neither too narrow, nor too broad—and apply the Clarity Compass to the subject of that more optimal scope. By managing the scope in this way, you'll be able to better close the gap between where you are and where you want to be.

One note here: Even though it is in my nature to frame each situation as an opportunity, and thereby create an "opportunity statement," the term that most of my clients best relate to is "problem statement." The client is always right, you know, so go ahead and create a specific problem statement to define the scope of the situation you're trying to improve.

Deck & Matilda

To help illuminate the sub direction of scope, we'll now return to Deck and Matilda. As we explore each case study, I encourage you to finish writing down your answers for your "Big Challenge" as you read through each sub direction. If a situation is particularly complex, potentially confrontational, or simply very important to you, it's worth taking the time to clarify things in writing. Writing often allows you to see a more complete picture, prompting you to continually return to what you originally wrote for reference or revision.

When you decide to approach paper with pen, remember that there is no one correct way to record your thoughts. In our case studies, for example, you will see that Deck wrote out his answers in a narrative format, whereas Matilda wrote hers in bulleted lists. Choose whatever format you are comfortable using. What is most important is that you capture as much information as you need in order to fully answer what each sub direction asks.

At the very least, for now, I urge you to write down the answers for your "Big Challenge." After working through this first Clarity Compass, I also encourage you to write out as many Clarity Compass situations as you can. By doing this you'll not only become faster with the tool, but you'll also become sharper in your thinking and more emotionally intelligent. Finally, as you develop a practice of writing through situations, you will find that your ability to make finer discernments, choices, and decisions will come more naturally to you in your daily on-the-spot encounters and conversations. You'll also learn to see when the full Clarity Compass is necessary, and when the Speed Clarity Compass will do!

Now let's see how Deck and Matilda, our two case studies, go about extracting the scope for their situations.

DECK

At the time of his first Clarity Compass coaching session, Deck was tearing his hair out. Even when I brought up the topic of his dogs, he remained visibly stressed. Deck was in no mood for small talk, and taking his cue, I moved forward with the business at hand.

"Let the structure guide you," I told him. "Define your problem's scope."

Deck was quick with his answer, scrawling out on a piece of paper:

- **I keep having to train new people. I don't understand why they keep leaving. The problem that I want to solve is that <u>my people are leaving too frequently</u>.**

Deck was surprised to note that the simple act of identifying his scope, or problem statement, in writing had already created a slight, but important shift. He noticed himself moving from the underlying repetitive belief, *People are ungrateful*, to a more level-headed and optimistic sentiment, *Here's a problem that definitely has a solution*.

MATILDA

Matilda preferred to write down her scope in the privacy of her own office and was resistant to using any methodology to think problems through. I thought of her former life as a competitive swimmer, and of mine. Although the world of competitive athletics is pretty rough and rarely "calm" or "quiet," when I found that magic pace, things settled. I let Matilda be, and she eventually came up with the following:

- **_Situation: I want to be selected as senior partner, but my not receiving exemplary reviews is preventing me from attaining the promotion._**
- **_Scope/Problem statement: Broader scope - I have not been chosen for senior partner. I keep being passed over due to subpar reviews._**

Matilda stopped and thought about it for a moment. This "Become Senior Partner" scope was much too broad for her to tackle right off the bat. She needed to narrow it down. Next she wrote:

- **Scope _for this Clarity Compass: Regardless of my high performance, Ling refuses to give me the good reviews I need to be chosen for senior partner._**

Part of working out a solution involved Matilda discovering that she was actually trying to solve a bunch of different problems at once. This over-complicated the issue and made the solution that much harder to see. By addressing each problem separately, Matilda was able to uncover the more specific root problem, prioritize where she put her energy, and build on her successes. The same process can apply when you realize that what you thought was a single Intention was actually several congruent Intentions. The key is to take each challenge in turn. It took time for them to develop, it will take time to understand and dismantle them.

As you use the Clarity Compass, you will likely revise

your scope, and find that depending on the way you frame it, the scope can actually move you toward or away from your desired outcome. If you are not careful, the way you frame the scope of a problem can actually misdirect your efforts. Sometimes, this causes you to avoid examining your Blind Spots, allowing you to sidestep the very thing you're trying to address.

For instance, when I worked with Matilda on her impressions about Ling, I found that she had a habit of not only looking at the situation in a way that was *not helping*, but that also exacerbated a number of issues. By telling herself, "Ling is not interested in my input. No matter what I do, he just isn't the sort of person to value other people's judgment," she was supporting herself in thinking that the problem was one hundred percent Ling's and that there was nothing she could do about it. Eventually, we were able to bring to her awareness that she too carried responsibility for the situation.

Her new scope read:

- **Scope/Problem statement: *Broader scope - I have not been chosen for senior partner, but I keep being passed over due to subpar reviews. Scope for this Clarity Compass – I'm not receiving the good reviews from Ling that I need in order to be chosen for senior partner.***

While the change in Matilda's scope may seem subtle, she had eliminated her bias and story from the original scope about Ling's refusal to give her good reviews and support her. This enabled her to begin to assume more accountability and figure out what she could do differently. As she became better at articulating her needs and expectations, as well as inquiring into Ling's, the door to a solution began to open.

Scope Case Study Wrap Up: Note how both Deck and Matilda experienced a shift in thinking once they had written down their scope. Gaining clarity on the scope of the problem brought about an openness to solutions and new attitudes.

Practicing the Sub Directions

In this first practice session on scope, and for all of the practice sessions that follow, I encourage you to discover and evaluate where there may be opportunities for improving your life. My assumption is that you will be working through your "Big Challenge" as you work through the book. That said, while your chosen challenge should be the focal point, the practices are an invitation to go beyond the one example of your "Big Challenge" and apply the material to new situations.

Remember that your Ego will love this type of discernment, because the Ego is driven toward providing you with greater control, safety, and comfort. But, you will also need to invoke your Heart in order to continue to embrace your life as it is, as well as to expand in a way that is courageous. This Ego-Heart duo is very empowering and yet, surprisingly subtle. Normally, because of its need for control, the Ego resists the Heart's ambiguity and courageous risk-taking to find meaning. But there are two primary ways that the Ego can engage with the Heart. The first is when the Ego is strong and healthy enough to surrender and serve the Heart. The second is when the Ego is given enough control as it steps out into more ambiguous, relational, and courageous territory. One of the primary intentions of the Clarity Compass is to provide a model, concepts, and practices that strengthen the Ego, as well as guide it along the path of serving the Heart, challenging Blind Spots, and upgrading Reality Maps.

One reason your Ego may not like the sub direction practices at first is because it thinks it already understands the Clarity Compass. If you've memorized the Two Polarities, your Ego may be saying, "I already understand this," especially if you've skipped ahead and memorized all the sub directions. However, the fact is that the Clarity Compass takes practice. It is more similar to playing the scales of the piano than it is to memorizing the periodic table. One of my clients who has taken it upon himself to teach the Clarity Compass to the leaders of his company said to me, "Brit, I really don't know the Clarity Compass."

I was surprised, so I replied, "It seems like the people you're teaching the Clarity Compass to use it effectively. How can it be that you don't know it?"

He quickly retorted, "I understand the Clarity Compass well enough to teach it. But I also know that that there are many more levels of understanding it that are available to me. And I can see skills available to me that I haven't even begun to practice."

My client wasn't shortchanging himself on the gifts that he did have with the Clarity Compass. He just had the humility to envision himself performing at even higher levels. The point is, even when you've reached certain levels of mastery in using the Clarity Compass for emotional intelligence and problem solving, there are still further levels to go if you practice.

Practicing Scope

In order to practice scope, first take some time to reflect on a new situation you know needs tending to. This could be a specific challenge you've been having at work or at home. You might want to work through an issue you are having with a supervisor or peer, a spouse, a sibling, or a child. Choose a situation that is long-term and ongoing, or one that just came up today, hold it in your mind, and then work through the following steps:

1. What is the problem statement that you have for the situation? Does it address what could be better?
2. Write down the scope of the problem.
3. Ask yourself whether this scope is part of a larger problem?
4. Does this scope contain or generate other problem statements?
5. Extra credit: Consider another situation you are currently facing and repeat the above steps.

Once you understand the scope of your intention, and have defined it in a clear, unambiguous problem statement, you will be able to articulate the next sub direction of the Intentions Direction, your desired outcome.

Desired Outcomes

While scope is about defining the problems you're facing, outcomes are about envisioning solutions or the end state that meets important needs. An outcome is a descriptive statement of your objectives—the more specific and quantifiable, the better. For example, Alexander agrees to take care of the dog on Tuesday nights, or the product is shipped by November 23rd with less than one percent error rate at a cost of less than four hundred and thirty thousand dollars.

Not all outcomes are quantifiable. For example, if the scope is "Sally and I are arguing frequently," the outcome may read as "Sally and I are getting along well." In cases such as these, try to at least come up with some measure of quantification. For example, try shifting from a scope of "Sally and I currently argue seventy percent of the time that we are talking, which is far more than I'm comfortable with," to an outcome of, "Sally and I argue forty five percent of the time that we are talking." At minimum, your desired outcomes will guide you in being able to say, "I have achieved this goal," or "I have a ways to go before I achieve this goal."

Some people are resistant to defining clear outcomes because it requires work. Other folks are resistant to defining clear outcomes because they are uncomfortable with accountability. Sometimes, desired outcomes can benefit both you and someone else. These are mutually beneficial outcomes (MBO). Whether it is a mutually beneficial or a personal outcome, refining your desired outcome will give your path a direction.

Write your scope as a problem statement and your outcome as a picture or vision of how the desired end state will look. Let's see how Deck and Matilda tackled their desired outcomes.

DECK

Deck's desired outcome seemed pretty simple:

- ***My employees stay for longer than the industry standard, contributing stability and the experience that they gain to the company and our clients.***

The most measurable part of this outcome lies in "exceeding the industry standard." Ideally the outcome can be measured or confirmed, but it's important not to become so rigid with the outcome that we become immobilized trying to create a measure. Remember, Deck just wanted to put in a good day's work, grow his company, and make a profit. His people had to know this already; it was part of the company's mission statement. So why weren't they staying and doing what they were being paid well to do?

Deck glared at the desired outcome on the page. He could have gone any number of directions with the impact of the written outcome, but at last he realized that he was incorrectly assuming that the biggest block to reaching this outcome was his employees' ingratitude. *"Let's suppose my people aren't ungrateful, and aren't deliberately trying to sabotage my business,"* he allowed himself to think. *"How am I off in my estimation of their motives? "*

MATILDA

Matilda's desired outcomes for this Clarity Compass were also fairly basic.

- ***Outcomes: I want to receive good reviews from Ling.***

She already knew that she wanted to get good reviews in order to become senior partner—this wasn't earth-shattering news to her. However, by writing her desires out on paper, Matilda's sense of motivation became sharper and her ideas for changing the way she worked and approached challenges came into focus. Now that she had written down specifically where she wanted to go, she felt more optimistic that her path to getting there would be clearer.

Desired Outcome Case Study Wrap Up: Note the optimism that Matilda gained and the shift in perspective that Deck underwent after simply writing down and reflecting on their desired outcomes. While writing out their outcomes brought up some negative beliefs they had about the others, it also pushed them to move past their limited and foggy beliefs and begin to focus on a positive, clear end state. Remember to work on your "Big Challenge" as you follow Deck and Matilda.

Practicing Outcomes

When diving into this practice, close your eyes and bring to mind the things you are most enthusiastic about. What would make you want to get up and tackle the challenges facing you? Practice outcomes by:

1. Thinking about and listing situations you can improve. Put simply: What situations make you want to pull the covers over your head for ten extra minutes in the morning? What situations make you want to hide in bed all day?

When you have the answers to these questions, continue to improve the chances that the outcomes of these situations *can and will* start to turn out more positive by:

2. Imagining alternative versions of those "I don't want to face the day" situations and envisioning a clear—and completely positive —outcome for each one. Picture an outcome that fills you with healthy energy and the will to act promptly.

Deeper Wants

Our deeper wants are the "Why" behind our outcomes. They are the driving force behind everything we do. Intentions underpin every aspect of the Clarity Compass, and deeper wants underpin our Intentions. Every goal we set, every decision we make, every project we start or conversation we have—each stems from a need or a want that we are trying to meet. To get a better sense of what your deeper wants are, consider the following questions:

- What moves me?
- What drives me?
- What do I hope to experience if things turn out well?

Deeper wants are deeply rooted in us. They include survival-based needs like food, water, shelter, and physical safety. They also include less tangible desires such as friendship, security, collaboration, fun, and meaning. As you become more aware of your needs and wants, you'll find that in any given situation, dozens could be at play.

Be aware that there are a multitude of deeper wants, such as: having a sense of control, achievement, community, creativity, respect, belonging, pride, job security, financial security, knowledge, contributing, superiority, wealth, peace, relief, free time, control (I mention control twice since it's such a big one), and so on.

Deeper wants can also be things you want to avoid, such as anxiety, failure, risk, and rejection; being wrong, fired, or disliked; and angering others or feeling stupid. Aversions such as these can often act as clues, directing you towards positive, deeper wants. The deeper wants that deal with inviting or avoiding situations are both powerful.

One of the best ways to begin to see how driven you are by wants is to pay attention to how many times throughout the day you speak the words "I want." Notice how frequently you process those two words inside your own head. We are born with wants, and certainly advertising and marketing geniuses are working ceaselessly to ensure our wants increase and are directed at their products. But, products are superficial and any desire for products stems from something deeper.

As we become more aware of our deeper wants, we begin to experience that which deeply moves us. We realize more fully what we are powerfully drawn to and what repels us. Our deeper wants can move us to create meaningful and fulfilling outcomes. At the same time, if our deeper wants are seeking fulfillment through unsavory outcomes, they can compel us toward creating outcomes that have miserable side effects. Even some of the positive outcomes we are trying to create can have disastrous ramifications if we are too attached to getting what we want. Most of the examples in this book are examples of good people with good Intentions becoming more attached to their own Intentions, as opposed to listening to the other person or opening up to their Blind Spots. Acknowledging and owning our deeper wants is essential for emotional intelligence and being effective in the world.

Situational Wants vs. Deeper Wants

One of the best practices in becoming aware of and owning our deeper wants is to begin to detach them from the particular situations that they come from. Most people are significantly challenged by this exercise. For example, when asked what their deeper want is, many of my clients will quickly say something like, "I want the team to succeed." But this is an example of an outcome, not a deeper want.

When I ask them to step back and try again by focusing on what they might personally gain from such an outcome (team success), they often say something like, "I want the team to succeed so that I can feel like I've accomplished something."

This second statement is closer to their deeper want, in that it helps to reveal their own personal investment in the team's success. But this "situational want" is still tied to the circumstances (the team's success) in which the deeper want is manifesting.

To get towards bedrock, I further encourage clients to separate their deeper want from any particular situation. At this point I usually hear something along the lines of: "I want to feel like I've accomplished something."

This third statement is a pure deeper want. Notice it doesn't have anything to do with the team, but focuses solely on the deeper want (and the "wanter") itself. As clients parse the deeper want from any given situation, they're able to take responsibility for their own wants and needs, and ultimately return to situations with greater clarity, resilience, focus and effectiveness.

As you can see from the example above, we can express our deeper wants purely without mentioning a particular situation or we can express our deeper wants within the context of the situation—a "situational want." The following examples are provided to support you in your practice of separating pure and simple deeper wants from situational wants:

Situational Wants contain a description of a desired outcome combined with a deeper want. Deeper wants contain only a description of the experience the person wants, without any reference to a particular situation or outcome. Once a deeper want is embedded in a situation, it is referred to as a situational want. Allow me to provide some examples of the difference between situational wants and deeper wants:

Harry has a great job and many solid friendships, but he has always felt something was missing in his life. A few months ago, he met Sarah and they began dating exclusively very quickly. With his 30th birthday approaching, Harry is starting to feel anxious about Sarah's feelings toward him, and he wants to figure out why. Things are going so well, so why is he plagued with self-doubt?

- Situational wants: *I want Sarah to love me.*
- Deeper wants: *I want to be romantically loved.*

Notice that as Harry sorts out the difference between situational wants and deeper wants, Sarah is left out of the deeper wants. Harry realizes that although he does love Sarah and wants to hear from her that she loves him too, the core issue is deeper than that. Growing up, not only was Harry an only child, but he was also somewhat neglected. His parents traveled frequently for business, and he was often left alone with the nanny. So even though he's not a serial dater and believes there is only a handful of people in the entire world each of us could be happy with, he also realizes that *if just somebody* loved him, his deeper want would be fulfilled.

Rita is an executive trying to better understand what is driving her. She has consistently been promoted and awarded throughout her career. She has been headhunted aggressively with bigger and bigger financial packages dangled in front of her. But overall, she feels unsettled and unsatisfied. She often finds herself nodding off in the middle of high-stakes meetings and daydreaming of a job with a title "grander" than her current one. In terms of her wants, she worked through to this:

- Situational want: *I want to be Vice President of International Operations to feel successful.*
- Deeper want: *I want to feel successful.*

Notice that the job title, VP of International Operations, is left out as Rita switches from situational wants to deeper wants. When she determines what her deeper want is, Rita actually broadens her possibilities for creating more success. She has liberated her need to feel successful from a particular job title. More importantly, as Rita sits with her need for success as defined outside of a job title, she is able to work more directly with the drive that exists inside her. She realizes no job title alone will ever satisfy her, and that her drive for success is insatiable. She has much soul-searching to do.

Rolf holds the same "desire" for an impressive work title, but with a different deeper want than Rita's. Rolf's want is more about what he demonstrates to the world, and less about an internal feeling of being successful.

- Situational want: *I want to be Vice President of International Operations to demonstrate achievement.*
- Deeper want: *I want to demonstrate to the world that I'm an achiever.*

What formed this need to be recognized for achievement in Rolf? As he begins to explore this question deeply, he might experience some discomfort, but ultimately, this self-knowledge will propel him closer to satisfying both his situational and deeper wants.

As Rolf shuffles through his deeper wants, he may find that, like Rita, he has an insatiable drive, or he may discover that his need to be recognized could be completely fulfilled by a particular title. There is no one answer as to what will truly satisfy a deeper want, but if we are too focused on the situation and not the deeper want, we might miss important information related to what drives us.

In sorting through the possible roots of what they need and want, many clients find great worth in looking at the values and circumstances of the family that they grew up in. They also find that once they begin to explore, acknowledge, and name their deeper wants, the wants reduce in intensity and seem to have less of a hold on them. From there, clients can manage their behaviors more effectively, which is the essence of emotional intelligence.

Deeper wants can always be further scrutinized. In any of these examples, one could ask themselves, "Is there a deeper want *beneath* my deeper want?" For example, underneath the desire to demonstrate achievement, there might be a deeper want to impress others or to be held in high esteem. There could be no end to this level of questioning, and it is entirely up to you to decide when you're done exploring and when you have discovered your own, more foundational, deeper wants.

It's also important to remember that situational wants are crucial in helping us to make the mental transition from outcomes to deeper wants. In my years of helping clients and course participants through significant life transformations, naming situational wants has been a necessary element of their progress. This is because almost everyone has such a difficult time transitioning from the *external* outcome to an *internal* deeper want that they experience as distinct from the situation they are exploring. The situational want provides a way of bridging the gap from the objective to the subjective.

With Matilda, for example, her ultimate outcome was to be promoted based on getting stellar performance reviews from Ling. The situational wants that Matilda could list were: "I want recognition from Ling; I want the senior partners to see me as an equal; I want my performance recognized by the company." The deeper wants could be: "I want recognition; I want to be seen as equal."

All of our desired outcomes are related to our deeper wants, but we are so focused on outcomes—saving money, gaining friends, finding a worthwhile career, making a gratifying purchase—that we are rarely aware of the many deeper wants underlying our moment-to-moment interactions and activities. In working with thousands of clients over thirty-five years, I have witnessed how challenging it is for people to access their deeper wants. They are so subtle, complex, or unattractive to us that they usually remain elusive.

As an extreme example, I recently worked with a client, Rob, who was having trouble with a colleague, Sally. Sally controlled an area upon which many of his deliverables were dependent, and Rob talked at length, and with much angst, about how irrational, controlling, and even vindictive she could be. He shared how uncooperative she was when he had given her a call that morning to try to move some of the issues forward. When I asked him what his intentions were for reaching out and calling her, he said, "I just wanted to call and see how I could help her."

As he was talking, I could see that Rob sincerely believed everything he was saying. Like many of us, he believed that one of his pure deeper wants was to be a helpful person. However, there wasn't much that Sally needed from him. In fact, he was primarily dependent on her. Upon further questioning, and to his bewilderment, he realized that he was trying to manage Sally primarily toward meeting *his goals*. Helping her out was a secondary intention. He shared that he was beginning to realize that he didn't actually care about helping her at all. He realized that his desire was to help her only so far as it helped him to meet his deeper wants. He wanted to feel competent and empowered.

Trying to influence someone who has control over important aspects of your work or personal life is a reasonable goal. Where Rob was running into trouble was in thinking and behaving as if he was doing Sally a favor by reaching out to help her. His disingenuous disposition was seeping into conversations he was having with Sally. As he assessed his own behavior more objectively, he decided that he was being inauthentic and manipulative. More importantly, he was able to distinguish between his situational and deeper wants. His situational wants concerned making his deliverables and getting Sally's cooperation. His deeper wants were to feel successful, effective, competent, empowered, and capable of achieving goals. As he dug even further, he realized he also liked having control and autonomy. The more he was driven by his deeper wants, the less aware he was of the degree to which they were driving him to be controlling and resentful of the situation with Sally.

Over time, Rob was able to admit to himself that because he resented Sally, he had developed a deeper want to experience empowerment through revenge. In addition, he developed a situational want to make her wrong, get revenge, and punish her for making his life so difficult.

You can see how unearthing and confessing to these last deeper and situational wants might cause us to squirm. It is sometimes unattractive to admit our deeper wants to ourselves, let alone to another person. Even some of our positive deeper wants, such as desiring connection or being helpful, can become detrimental if we become more attached to the outcome than we realize. However, once these powerful and influential deeper wants are brought into awareness, they influence us less compulsively and more productively.

I frequently share with my clients Carl Jung's notion that autonomous parts of the psyche have more power over us than the parts that are integrated. This means that there are many parts of our mind that influence our thinking and behavior, and the less conscious and integrated these parts are, the greater the impact they will have on our lives. Let me explain this through the lens of the Clarity Compass. If our deeper wants remain in our unconscious and influence us autonomously, they will affect our lives more than the deeper wants we have consciously acknowledged and integrated.

Deeper wants are about what matters most to you as a human being, independent of any institution, job title, or team of people. Stay with yourself. We're not making situational wants bad. Again, if a *situational want* starts to creep in as you are listening for deeper wants, jot it down and refocus. I suggest to my clients that they write out their situational wants. As I've already mentioned, when asked for deeper wants, clients often find it challenging to get past the first thing that comes to mind. For example, "I want to make my bonus of one hundred and fifty thousand dollars." Statements such as this one are about the situation, and though valuable, you want to get past them. Beneath this one hundred and fifty thousand dollar marker is the statement: "I want financial security," or "I want financial freedom." Or even, "I want recognition," or "I want the feeling of reaching my goals."

Deck and Matilda, like many clients, found the situational/deeper want exercise challenging at first. Like many of us, they are short on time and unaccustomed to such focused self-examination. Scratching beneath the surface to bring about real and lasting change requires setting a few other tasks aside, but as you now know, it's worth it!

Let's look at how Deck & Matilda explored their own wants.

DECK

Deck found himself anchored in how annoying it felt to be left in the lurch by so many employees leaving so frequently, so he continued to dig deeper. After much work and scrutiny, he came up with the following:

- **Situational want:** *I want people to produce services and profits for me.*
- **Deeper want:** *I want prosperity. I want ease. I want to feel respected. I want to be obeyed.*

Many clients might be put off by the realization that they want to be obeyed, since they normally have never considered themselves as controlling. Deck's military experience showed him that the man in control is the man who sees his will carried out. But in his non-military work situation, he had been discovering that no matter how many orders he issued, there was no guarantee he would see results. It made him feel out of sync with the whole world, which in turn made him feel vulnerable—a sensation he loathed. His deeper wants were definitely not being met.

MATILDA

Matilda realized that though she very much wanted to be senior partner and get good reviews, she was uncomfortable writing down her deeper wants.

- **Deeper wants:** *I want to be seen as successful. I want to feel competent.*

Since she was already successful and competent, she didn't like thinking that she wanted to be seen as even more so, or that somehow she wasn't taking ownership of her success and competence. She also realized how much she hated the very act of questioning her worth, on both counts.

Deeper Wants Case Study Wrap Up: Note how uncomfortable digging into their deeper wants was for both Deck and Matilda. This is expected, but remember what I said about alarms: When a buzzer goes off in your head and tells you what you are about to write down is awful, shameful, annoying, arrogant, selfish, stubborn, or just plain "wrong," pay attention. Chances are you've unearthed a chance to make great strides toward personal and/or professional transformation. Just buckle your seat belt!

My clients tend to spend the bulk of their time identifying problems and solutions rather than listening to their underlying needs. We resist acknowledging our deeper wants because they can make us feel fragile, and at other times, repulsive. Being vulnerable can trigger a fear response. If we are weak, we are open to attack. Since we would rather avoid feeling the negative impact of exploring our deeper wants, we often try to meet our needs without acknowledging them, even to ourselves. But think about it—how can you fulfill a need if you have not quite defined or outlined what it is?

Greater awareness of the wide range of our deeper wants helps us to avoid being driven by the wants that aren't healthy for us, and it supports us in following wants that can bring forth healthier more meaningful outcomes. In my experience, the often-painful journey of examining deeper wants pays off with incredible insight, greater emotional intelligence, and mastery in one's life and joy.

Practicing Deeper Wants

You might guess by the presence of the word "deeper" that unless you're willing to move beyond the surface of things, you won't go far in improving or updating your Reality Maps. At first, going deeper may take more time than you expect, but the more you practice unearthing what you really want, the faster your archaeological missions to find and eliminate Blind Spots will become.

1. Think of a new situation where you feel more physical, mental, or emotional investment or disturbance than usual. Or, if you haven't already considered your "Big Challenge," use it.
2. Explore the three questions mentioned below, in relation to the situation:
   a. What moves me?
   b. What drives me?
   c. What do I hope to experience if things turn out well?
3. Without any judgement, spend the most time with the third question above, exploring in as much concrete detail as possible the experience you are hoping for.
4. Try to isolate the experience from the situation in order to focus only on the deeper wants as they

exist in you. For example, "I want security," "I want recognition," "I need peace," or "I deeply want love."

5. Again without judgment, notice how these deeper wants are influencing how you are thinking and behaving in the situation. Various deeper wants may be impacting you differently. For example, your desire for <u>security</u> might drive you toward increasing your financial success, while conversely, wanting <u>peace</u> might move you away from taking risks with projects or meetings. This might be the case even as your need for <u>recognition</u> might be urging you to speak out more.

Practicing the Intentions Direction

Now that we've explored scope, outcomes, and deeper wants, you likely have a pretty good sense of what the Intentions Direction is all about. Now, let's take some time to put it all into practice.

1. The next time you have a conversation, ask yourself, "Why am I speaking now?" and try to listen to what motivates you to say the things that you're saying. Try taking a few mini breaks throughout the day to reflect on the conversations you've had, and note the Intentions that prompted those conversations.

2. In your next few conversations, practice sharing your Intentions. Try to clearly articulate the outcome you're pursuing with your conversation partner and explain why that outcome is important to you.

3. Note some of the deeper wants you have noticed bubbling to the surface during these conversations.
4. Ask yourself if your Intentions are truly addressing your deeper wants.
5. Writing Practice: If you haven't already done so, reflect on your "Big Challenge." Using the questions in the sub direction practices above, write out a few sentences clearly defining scope, desired outcomes, and deeper wants.
6. Extra credit: Consider another situation you are currently facing. Write out a few sentences on scope, desired outcome, and deeper wants.

The Actions Direction

In the Clarity Compass, Intentions are nothing without Actions. Actions are the vehicle through which we make our Intentions manifest in the world. When I talk about Actions however, I'm not referring to "activity," as in the tasks and duties that fill your day. I've seen people fill their hours attending to minutia rather than diving into things that could really change their lives or help move their work or relationships forward. The Actions I'm talking about are the ones that have a real impact on the trajectory of our lives. Let me share a simple example.

I once watched a friend's seven-year-old, Sean, play soccer. About a third of the way through the game, I was impressed: "Wow, Sean is right there. He's in on almost every play!" However, around two-thirds of the way through the game my observation had changed to: "Sean is in on almost every play of the game, but he never actually kicks the ball."

There are many ways that we are in on the plays of life, but not really kicking the ball. Truly kicking the ball requires much more energy, skill, and especially risk than just being close in on a play.

The same is true of Actions. We may have clearly articulated and powerfully felt Intentions, but converting them into impactful Actions often takes imagination and effort, especially if we aren't paying attention to which Actions would create the most change. As an innocent child, Sean thought he was making a difference by placing himself in the middle of each play, but the truly *leveraged* Action—kicking the ball— understandably eluded him. As adults, let's compassionately wake up to where we are not kicking the ball in our own life.

The Lever

Archimedes said, "Give me a lever long enough, and a fulcrum on which to place it, and I shall move the world."

This declaration spurs us to find creative actions that will heavily impact our ability to achieve the results we seek. Archimedes' lever represents the essence of the Actions Direction. We seek highly leveraged Actions in order to make an impact in our home, office, or larger community. In Actions mode, we shift ourselves even further from the automaton end of the imagination continuum and move toward envisioning highly leveraged actions and having Creative Conversations.

Leveraged Action steps are the essence of the Actions Direction in that they contain the potential to produce a maximum outcome, especially in relationship to the effort we need to put in. You may be familiar with the 80/20 Rule, which states that eighty percent of our efforts bring about twenty percent of our results, meaning that we put great effort into achieving minimal results. That's a little disheartening, isn't it? But the good news is that the other twenty percent of our effort achieves eighty percent of our results. If we are discerning enough, we can gain significant results through minimal effort.

The essence of leveraged Action steps means that we seek out more opportunities where twenty percent of our effort will create eighty percent of our results, and we minimize the number of things that require eighty percent effort for twenty percent results. Of course, this increases our overall net effectiveness. There will always be the bottom twenty percent of "stuff to do" that requires the eighty percent extra effort, but as we learn to scale our effort with leveraged action steps, even that eighty percent extra effort will become more effective. I've seen hundreds of people turn the 80/20 Rule on its head by applying Archimedes' lever and their imaginations to come up with whole new sets of leveraged Actions. They have outdone themselves, and every time they do, they leverage more and sweat less.

In the Clarity Compass, the Actions/Intentions Polarity is grounded in the principle that we are most effective when we act from a place of deliberate Intention. Holding on to an Intention without setting it in motion tends to feel unsatisfying, while Action taken without a real direction usually misfires. The more your Intentions drive your Actions, the more effective you will be—so take the time to work on alignment. Leveraged Action steps are those consciously chosen Actions that will have the greatest impact in moving you toward what you want. They can range from making a request you might not have considered before to having the risky conversation you've resisted for years. They are the choices, big and small, that have the power to create the most positive, fulfilling change.

Inter-Action

In the mid-1980s, I was surprised to discover that one of the criteria for being defined as a scientist was that the researcher had to share information with the larger community. At first, I objected, stating that a person could technically conduct all the experiments they wished in the confines of their own laboratory and still be a successful and legitimate scientist. But over time, I came to understand the rationale behind the criteria: Because we are social beings, a true scientist is one that shares knowledge with others. We exist in community. We falter and thrive depending on our interactions with people.

Leveraged Actions entail working with and through people as opposed to using people to get what you want. Leveraged Actions rely on identifying the people who might be available for mutual collaboration and support. You may not be able to contribute much to the other person at the moment, but as long as you are willing, and even eager, to do so in the future, there is a give and take. The leveraged Action steps that appear in the Clarity Compass are those that move situations forward more quickly than other options.

While we typically focus on Actions that involve at least one other person, from time to time we may review some of our non-interaction based Actions, such as writing a report, creating a PowerPoint presentation, taking time for personal retreat, or blocking off time for a meditative strategy building session. These are all legitimate Actions, and some of them might also be leveraged Action steps. However, because the focus of the Clarity Compass is always on finding the places where your Reality Maps can shift in ways that allow you to gain greater traction or leverage in the world, most of the time this requires engaging with other people.

Even blocking off time for solo activities usually requires negotiation with other people. The point is, that ultimately, we create our lives through the kinds of conversations we have with people, as well as the particular people we choose as our conversation partners. We are social beings.

The Three Sub Directions of Actions

How can you stop running up and down that soccer field like a kicker with his head cut off and manage your Actions more effectively? How can you coordinate your Actions so that they are more tightly aligned with your Intentions and also more in line with the visions, goals, and Actions of your teammates? Using the three sub directions for the Actions Direction—requests, crucial people, and Creative Conversations—will help!

As you work through this section, keep in mind your previously identified "Big Challenge."

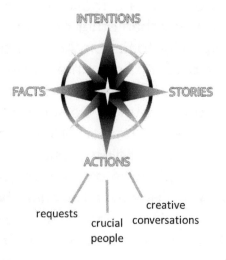

Requests

No one is on an island. To some extent, we are all dependent on one another. Requests are a reflection of living as socially interdependent human beings. The most effective requests are those that are linked directly to our Intentions. Requests range from the simple ("Could you please pass the salt?") to the interpersonally complex ("Can we talk about our argument yesterday?"). While making requests may be more difficult for some people than it is for others, I find that almost everybody can improve their ability to clearly articulate what they need and want.

Once we begin to scratch the surface of our Reality Maps, we can see how limited the perspectives they provide are. It then hits us that we have been going along through much of our lives with a skewed understanding of how clear our requests have been. It's easy to think we have made a request when, in fact, we have merely offered an opinion or shared a need without truly asking anyone for help. I have caught myself often saying to employees, "Gosh, I am so behind," and realizing later that my intention was to get them to step up and take care of tasks I didn't have time for. I assumed that they would know, or "it would hit them," that jumping in to lend a hand would be the best way to help out. Unchecked, these types of assumptions would leave me disappointed or frustrated. The fact is, my employees have busy lives of their own and I can't expect them to consistently interpret my vague statements as requests for Action. Remember the popular adage: *I'm not a mind reader!* Nobody is.

To make your requests both clear and actionable, try introducing them in a way that solicits a response, using phrases like, "Would you be willing to...?", "Is it doable for you to...?", or "Are you up for...?"

Use whatever phrases feel right for your personality, but avoid ambiguous phrases that state your desires without soliciting a clear response, such as, "I'd love it if you...", "I really hope that...", or "It would be great if..."

To test if the request you are making is clear, ask yourself if the listener is compelled to respond with some version of "yes" or "no." If not, then you probably need to improve your request game.

Similarly, requests that have no specific Actions associated with them can be too vague to be acknowledged or completed. Requests like, "Can you please be a little tidier?", "Are you up for spending more time together?", or "Would it be possible for you to be a bit more patient with our daughter?" don't give the recipient a clear Action to complete, and therefore don't usually result in an achievement you can acknowledge. Instead, actionable requests should clearly name a specific Action, with an achievable end-point. For example:

- Please, pass the salt.
- Would you meet with me at three o'clock on Tuesday?
- Will you take over the McGovern project?
- Will you take out the trash every Tuesday night?
- When our daughter is doing her math homework, could you give her thirty more minutes to complete the assignment?

Many of us also suffer from the requests we never make at all. We avoid asking for help for a multitude of reasons. For example: we believe we will come across as weak; we don't want to be an inconvenience; we don't want to feel obligated; we don't want others to resent us; we don't know we can be helped; or we don't want to give tasks to others who we believe are already overworked. In the end, by never even venturing to make a request, we often end up feeling overwhelmed, blaming others for not helping (even though we didn't ask them to), or channeling our energy in places that serve no one.

For instance, a friend once shared how frustrated she was that her children and husband rarely helped her wash dishes. "I have a full-time job and I prepare almost all the meals! The least they could do is wash a few dishes!" I listened to her, and after empathizing, I asked if she had ever requested their help. "Oh, they know I need help," she asserted.

I nudged her a little more. We looked together at what had actually been said and done, and she slowly realized that she had always simply assumed her family members knew she wanted help with washing up, although she had never explicitly asked. She finally made the direct request, "Please help me by washing a few dishes. You can take turns throughout the week." Her family began to pitch in after nearly every meal.

This may seem like a trivial example to some, but to my friend it was a tremendous change in her home and family experience. Change doesn't always come about radically, but if you don't ask for help—clearly and precisely—things are unlikely to change at all.

Another one of my clients, Richard, was feeling resentful of his office team members for not picking up tasks associated with a particularly important project. After spending some time on a Clarity Compass, he ended up laughing at himself and realized that while he expected his people to step into a variety of leadership roles on the project, he had never communicated these expectations to anyone. In fact, the problem was not that Richard's requests weren't clear and specific enough. He had never made any requests at all!

Why were my friend and Richard so hesitant to clearly state their requests? People tend to be hesitant about clearly stating their requests for a number of reasons, but the most common is that we fear we might create a negative or pressured environment. And while it *is* important to care about the impact of your requests on others, it's just as important to advocate for your own needs or the needs of others that you are responsible for. It's okay to balance advancing your own causes with being mindful of other people's boundaries and limitations. Don't forget that sharing your concerns for other people's wellbeing is always an option, particularly if you're worried a request will be too difficult or will make them feel obligated. People respond to authenticity. So put yourself out there. Ask for what you want and share what's true for you.

A final important aspect of making requests is making sure that they are stated in such a way that the other person truly wants to say "yes." Delivering compelling requests can take you much further—much faster—than you've ever imagined.

For now, let's see how Deck and Matilda formulated their clear and actionable requests:

DECK

Deck had always been a man of action. His sweat-free and wrinkle-free exterior hid very well a man who could not sit still—he would begin to pace if he sensed a lull in the action.

He was excited to finally move past some of what he had called the more "cerebral" or "touchy-feely" aspects of the Clarity Compass, and start thinking of "things he might *do*." He started by asking himself: What clear, actionable requests could I make to help improve my situation?

- ***I will ask the next employee who leaves for the opportunity to address their concerns, whatever they may be.***

Deck's sense of pride clamored against this idea. *If someone wants to desert, it's about their character, not mine.* But this problem was seriously affecting his company's bottom line. If he had to push his pride back in service of the greater good, then so be it. For Deck, it is celebration-worthy that he decided to make himself vulnerable enough to commit to requesting that a departing employee share their concerns and speak with him about the ways he could be more accommodating.

MATILDA

Matilda reflected back over the past few weeks, looking at the interactions she'd had with Ling and what had actually been said and done. She knew that much of their relationship was colored by her own anxieties, and came up with the following requests in her attempt to move the situation forward towards her desired outcome:

- **I will ask Ling to share with me if there's anything in particular I need to focus on to improve my performance review.**
- **I will ask Ling if he would be willing to re-evaluate my performance review.**

In setting out these requests, Matilda began to see how strong the gap was between what she wanted her relationship with Ling to be and what it truly was. Something about that gap rubbed her the wrong way. She could feel herself growing annoyed. She thought, "Why isn't Ling the kind of boss he should be?" She realized that part of her annoyance was that she did not like having to ask. She assumed that "it was already part of his job to give particular feedback and think of doing a re-evaluation." However, the more she thought about it, the more she realized that her reactivity was around being resistant to make requests. Asking for something

DR. BRIT POULSON

made her feel weak, vulnerable, and somehow at risk. But in the absence of asking, she was definitely not getting what she wanted.

Requests Case Study Wrap Up: Note the different feelings that making requests triggered in Matilda and Deck. See how important it was for them to decide on what specific requests to make. The requests are important in and of themselves, but it is equally important for us to note the impact that just thinking about making them can have on us.

Practicing Requests

When practicing requests, it's important to start simple. Ask yourself in the middle of a conversation, "What is it that I want from the other person? What would I like them to do?" As your requests become clearer in your own mind, verbalize them. Keep your requests **clear** and **actionable**. In addition, work on:

1. Noticing small, unaddressed or outlying wants or needs. Have you been waiting for someone to answer a question you haven't asked? How long have you been putting off making an appointment or calling in for customer service? Do you need assistance preparing or clearing up dinner, or in setting up or leading a meeting?
2. Watching how you ask for what you want. Are you being as clear and compelling as you need to be? Also, consider how appropriately polite, engaging, present, and personable you are being around the request. Notice where you're not being polite, as

well as where you are being *so polite* that people are not hearing your request (because it is getting lost in all the politeness).

3. Look for more opportunities to practice asking for something with greater clarity and in a more inviting and compelling manner.

Crucial People

We all operate within a number of networks, those webs of relationship that make up our personal, family, and work lives. Within these overlapping communities are individuals that I like to call "crucial people." These are people who could powerfully contribute to our effectiveness and help us achieve our desired outcomes.

You know what they say about how opening one door, leads to another? The same is true regarding the opening of the floodgates for more crucial people. Crucial people could either be folks we already know who are hiding in plain sight, or people we have yet to meet. We just need to start opening our eyes to the possibilities. By identifying and engaging with our crucial people, we can bring forth an untapped ocean of support, rather than being satisfied with the trickle of support we are currently receiving.

You probably have connections that really serve you, but for whatever reason, you haven't pursued them. People tend to dismiss connecting with a potentially helpful person because their Ego has created predetermined Stories that dismiss the potential helpfulness of this person, or that exaggerate the negative things that might happen: "I'll be bothering them," "I'll never get access to them," "I might be rejected or judged by them,"

"They might be annoyed or even angry with me," and so on. Our Ego's protectiveness prevents us from truly un-furling our sails for adventures that we could have with some crucial people. Ego constructs our Reality Maps in such a way that some of our most crucial people go uninvited to the journey because they don't even occur as "possible persons" who could make a difference in our lives.

So how do we identify the crucial people in our lives? Begin by first listing the names of people you'll need to consult as you pursue your outcome from the Intentions Direction. These names will probably come from your current circle of friends, community members, and colleagues. The more key people you have relationships with, the more opportunities you'll uncover. The more diverse and far-reaching your network, the greater access you'll have to the specific knowledge, skills, and support you need. Start to note people who aren't currently in your network, but could be.

While expanding your network is an important part of the crucial people sub direction, it is equally important that you look across the horizon of all the people you can think of and identify who you need to have a conversation with as soon as possible. Time is of the essence while you are expanding your support crew. Ask your-self, "If I'm taking the most leveraged actions, who would I be talking to right now?"

While you might be nervous about reaching out to the crucial people in your network, it rarely hurts to be gen-uinely friendly and inquisitive about other people. Re-member, most people don't bite! By stretching yourself, you stand to gain some incredible allies and collabora-tors.

Let's see how Deck and Matilda went about identifying their crucial people.

DECK

Deck, at first, joked, "Crucial *people*? Who am I kidding? Dogs are man's best friend." But of course, in working up his list, he knew he had to buckle down and leave his dogs out of the equation. The first crucial two-legged creature that came to mind was his older brother, Glen. Deck had always found him to be a good listener and someone he could trust with personal information and rely on for support.

- ***I will call Glen for personal advice, clear direction, and moral support.***

Another leader in his field, Joe, had a reputation as a good boss, something Deck had never taken seriously until now.

- ***I will set up a lunch with Joe for tips on leadership and talent development and retention.***

Deck knew there were probably more influential players to add to his list, but for now, having these two names down on paper gave him an immediate feeling of relief, support, and direction. Remember that while working through your Clarity Compasses, you will meet short-term and long-term goals—and sometimes, the most critical goal is immediate motivation to keep doing the hard work!

MATILDA

Matilda pondered who she might bring in as crucial people. With her history of always wanting to be Number One in the water, she understood the influence her swim coaches had had on her success. She also reflected on the ways in which it really did take a community to support athletes at her level. Her parents, for example, had consistently given up their free time to drop her off at early morning swim practices. A friend's mother would drive them to out of state competitions. It hit Matilda that perhaps she could look around her office and pull together a similar network. She noticed that she was less hesitant to ask for support because she knew that she would be willing to help out anybody in the office who asked her for support.

She considered two key senior partners she trusted and found approachable, Jake and Marlo. Neither were direct superiors, and they'd known Ling for years. Matilda also added Carson and Felicia, colleagues who had come up the ranks alongside her.

Once Matilda drew up her crucial people list, she felt lighter. She hadn't realized how solid her network actually was, and in seeing the names of these key players, she felt much more confident that she would find the support and advice she needed.

Crucial People Case Study Wrap Up: Note the relief that both Deck and Matilda felt just by acknowledging that they did indeed have people to go to for support. In these case studies, neither of them expressed feeling nervous about reaching out to the crucial people they listed. This might be the case for you too. However, many clients do end up listing a few people they are hesitant about contacting for a variety of reasons. You might also find that for some situations you work through, the crucial people list come more easily, while others present more of a challenge. That's normal—keep going!

Practicing Crucial People

It is rare for a person to accomplish great things solo. It truly does take a village. Build a network or support system for short and long-term situations by thinking carefully through the following steps:

1. Assuming you have a "to do" list, review it. Ask yourself, "Who are the crucial people I need to engage?"
2. Based on your "to do" list, make a list of four to six people you could develop a worthwhile relationship with that could help you out. "Worthwhile" is defined here as "mutually beneficial," whether on a professional or personal level.
3. Is your list missing an important support person? Are you avoiding someone? Have you considered adding someone you currently don't know to the list?
4. Place a star by two people you see as having the most potential to benefit you right now or as soon as possible.
5. For each of these starred people ask yourself: What requests do I need to make? Is there a request I am avoiding? How do I best engage them?
6. Reach out to those starred people. Once you have read through the Clarity Compass, you can let it

guide you further in how to reach out to each specific person, but for now, if you're feeling confident in your approach toward an individual, simply go for it!

Creative Conversations

I have seen clients use the Clarity Compass in a multitude of ways, toward the achievement of all sizes and types of goals, shifts, and transformations. As you work your way through your first Reality Maps and Blinds Spots, you'll discover the many ways the Clarity Compass influences your life. For me, one of the main benefits of using the Clarity Compass is the "Creative Conversations" that it encourages me to engage in. Creative Conversations are constructive communications where the Clarity Compass and imagination are directly applied with the intention of generating new and better outcomes.

As social beings, we construct the content of our lives through the choices we make in our social engagements. More concretely, we create our lives through the conversations that we choose to have, and choose not to have. We then choose to further create and engage depending on:

1. Who we choose to talk with.
2. What we choose to say.
3. What we choose not to say.
4. How we choose to say it.

The types of conversations that we choose to engage in, or to avoid, are largely influenced and determined by our Reality Maps. Often, we believe we are making our best effort to move conversations forward, and typically blame any lack of cooperation or understanding on the other person. If our conversation did not bring us the expected results, we think, mostly at an unconscious level, "It must be them, not me, because again, I'm doing the best I can." But this self-confirmation comes from Blind Spots and the Ego's insistence on being right. If we can use our imagination to open up to new possibilities for how to interact with the other person, we can take more responsibility for a particular situation, and by extension take more responsibility for our lives. We become more empowered.

Unleashing Your Creativity through Conversations

The Clarity Compass is less about how to use a particular phrase to be more persuasive, and more about owning our part of the creative nature of our conversations. Of course, at first it is difficult to do this consciously, since most of our conversations are driven by unconscious assumptions based on our unconscious and conscious Reality Maps.

While all conversations are creative in the sense that we are creating our lives through them, I am reserving the phrase "Creative Conversations" for those where we are intentionally trying to create a different dynamic by consciously paying attention to the Reality Maps that are driving the conversations. The Clarity Compass helps us to systematically examine the most critical aspects of a situation in order to draw out the larger belief systems within our Reality Maps from which the situation is born. As we begin to explore more details of a situation and to then figure out how they relate to the bigger Clarity

Compass picture, we discover alternate perspectives and more creative ways to move the situation forward toward the goals we hold most valuable.

If we are stuck in our Reality Maps' biases and operating from Blind Spots, we begin to calcify, killing off any possibility for achieving beneficial outcomes. Creative Conversations are the cure to such rigidity. The best way to begin thinking about having a Creative Conversation is to bring the Clarity Compass and your imagination into a situation in order to bring out the best possible outcome.

In many situations, you won't need to launch into a Creative Conversation. For example, if my green beans are somewhat tasteless (scope/problem statement), I want more flavor (outcome), so I'd simply make the request, "Please, pass the salt." In this interaction, the Intentions to Action Polarity is as clear as a bell. It's not necessary to go into my deeper wants, the crucial person is probably the closest to the salt, and I don't have to have a Creative Conversation. In simple situations, the Intentions to Action Polarity is enough.

If you're like most people though, you have to engage with people not just around the dinner table. You often have to deal with situations much more complicated than being presented with a pile of tasteless green beans. You have family members or coworkers that have different priorities, communication styles, agendas, or simply conflicting roles and perspectives. Creative Conversations are typically essential in these highly complex or volatile situations, and therefore often require going through the Facts versus Stories Polarity first. For this reason, we will revisit the Creative Conversations sub direction after we've gone through Facts versus Stories

Polarity.

By now, I'm hoping you are looking forward to seeing how Deck and Matilda apply each sub direction to the situation. We will include their case studies in a separate chapter on Creative Conversations at the end of our learning about Clarity Compass for Self.

Practicing Creative Conversations

We will practice Creative Conversations in more depth after we examine the Facts versus Stories Polarity. For now, notice how you are thinking and behaving in important conversations by asking yourself the following questions:

1. What are my Intentions for the conversation itself?
2. How collaborative am I being?
3. How open am I to solutions and outcomes that are creative, but previously not imagined or put forward?
4. How open am I to having a different kind of conversation with this person than I have previously had with them? What different kinds of conversations can I imagine as a possibility, and what might they be able to imagine or dream up that I can't (not through any fault or weakness of my own, but simply because of the perspective my Reality Maps and Blind Spots offer)?

Play with these questions now. They will help you to deepen your understanding and increase your skills when we revisit Creative Conversations.

Practicing the Actions Direction

Now that you've had a chance to explore requests, crucial people, and creative conversations, it's my hope that you're starting to intuit a way of interacting and living that will super-charge your effectiveness and relationships by learning to take conscious, leveraged actions. After walking through each sub direction and its associated practice, we can weave all three sub directions together into one practice:

1. If you haven't already done so, recall your "Big Challenge" and write out a few sentences for requests, crucial people, and Creative Conversations.
2. Beyond your "Big Challenge," practice making simple requests. Ask yourself in the middle of a conversation, "What is it that I want from the other person? What would I like them to do?" As your request becomes clear, make it. Keep it **clear** and **actionable**.
3. Identify two people to add to your network, and articulate to yourself how you could help each other.
4. Assuming again that you have a to-do list, find one thing on the list that you planned on doing yourself, but will now request that someone else do it. Notice what this suggestion and your subsequent requests kicks up for you in terms of fairness, responsibility, or asking for support.
5. Extra credit: consider another situation you are currently facing. Write out a few sentences for requests, crucial people, and Creative Conversations.

Summary of the Intentions to Actions Polarity

The Intentions to Actions Polarity is the more organic of the Two Polarities, as acting on an Intention is—from birth—the natural outcome of wanting anything. From restlessness to nourishment to emotional comfort, we feel a need and we act to address it. This also fits with the old adage: *Why, What, and How?* "Why?" is always the first question we should ask when we set out to do anything. The *Why* relates to scope and deeper wants. "What?" hones in on what we want, based on our answers to the *Why* question. The *What* refers to outcomes. "How?" is what we do to get something done in relation to the *Why* and *What*. Therefore, it refers to the entire Actions Direction.

Think of the toddler who sees that big soft teddy bear on the toy store shelf and throws a temper tantrum in the aisle if Mom says "no" until their need for something button-eyed and fluffy to hug is met.

Of course, adult life is generally more complex, and throwing a tantrum to get what we want (as much as we might want to at times) isn't exactly an effective strategy. To address those wants, we must participate in a more complicated world. But the essential link remains the same: We discern a need, and we act to fill it, often by having a Creative Conversation that includes making well-formed requests of the crucial people in our networks. For a couple of simple examples, I might ask a friend, "Will you drive me to the airport?" You might ask a colleague, "Can you explain the steps you're planning to take with this project?"

Inherent within each of these requests is an Intention and an end Action. The Clarity Compass helps us stay aware of how we are mapping the terrain and plotting our path from these separate points, through the many interactions and Creative Conversations we have throughout our lives. At the end of the day, the only way to meet our goals is to actually take the leveraged steps that will bring us to where we want to be. If we are in that soccer game, but only showing up and running back and forth, it's ultimately not enough. We have to kick the ball!

CHAPTER **4**

Facts versus Stories:
The East West Polarity

The Difference between Facts and Stories

Most of us are aware that a chasm divides the way we perceive the world from the way it actually is. It's impossible to see the world perfectly, without distortion. Just think about how much clearer we are today than our ancestors were about certain truths of the physical world. We're amused, for example, at the fact that not too long ago, most humans believed the Earth was flat. So it shouldn't be hard to imagine what humans one hundred years from now may think about us—how foolish, how naïve they were! (Actually, at the pace we're moving, those who are ten to fifteen years younger

79

already experience a significant gap in their understanding of the world, compared to their "elders." Just start talking to them, as I often do, about all this new troublesome technology!). From a historical perspective to modern day, no one can see an objective world perfectly, clearly, and accurately.

With the Clarity Compass, we explore the chasm between the world as it is and the world as we perceive it. That gap is created by the number of Blind Spots we have in our Reality Maps.

The first step in transcending our own subjectivity is to focus on what we can actually know: Facts. Facts are those things that can be objectively observed; they cannot be disputed. For example, whatever you see in front of you in this moment can largely be considered as Fact. If there's a pen in front of you, that's a Fact. If you watch someone pick up the pen, it's a Fact that you saw them pick up the pen.

Stories, on the other hand, are things we believe, and for which we have no original, first-hand proof. Beliefs tend to be supported by a few Facts (sometimes very few, sometimes a great many), and the more Facts that support a belief, the more likely it is that that the belief hews close to reality. For example:

Fact: Geneva spilled her coffee on her blouse.

Story: Geneva is careless; or, the spill was bound to happen since she drank so much coffee; or, she was looking for an excuse to leave the office and acted intentionally.

Whereas, the Intentions to Actions Polarity highlights the <u>flow</u> from being purposeful to leveraged activity, the Facts vs. Stories Polarity highlights the <u>difference</u> between something that is observed and that which is interpreted. So in this chapter, we want to learn how to distinguish between the objective events in our experience and how we subjectively perceive them.

Why is this distinction so important? During my doctoral studies in cognition at Georgia State University, my professor, James Pate, drilled into me the difference between *empirical data* and *theoretical interpretations*. Scientists have to know the difference between the data they are observing and the conclusions they are drawing from those observations, right? If they aren't clear on this, we question the validity of their research, their claims, or their findings.

I invite you to be a scientist of your own life.

Because when we rely so heavily on our Stories, we make mistakes. We lose the ability to interact with the world as it actually is, so we create chaos, cloud our decision-making process, and miss out on important opportunities. If you want better results, you need to have a solid grip on the Facts of a situation, and you need to be aware of where you are making assumptions. Which of your Stories are you erroneously calling Facts?

The Facts Direction

Before setting off on a Fact-collecting mission, consider what your basic video camera does: It simply records what it sees. It makes no judgments about other people, and their motives, Intentions, or Actions. *A man walks into a store, and then out again, putting his lips to a bottle in a bag.* That's it. We may want to make up a story about what is in the bag, why it is in the bag, why he is drinking from the bottle in the bag, or whether he is really drinking anything at all. But that's all Story.

In many ways, our five senses are meant to work like a video camera. We see and hear things in our surroundings, and we remember them. We are sometimes moved to Action based on what we see, and sometimes not. Our minds can bring us both Facts and Stories, but we can (and must) consciously and continuously retrain ourselves to regulate the lens—to better separate Facts from Stories. Doing so will give us the clearest possible picture of any situation, which will ultimately aid us in our quest to make better choices.

The primary intention of the Facts Direction is to ground us in the reliability of Facts over the Stories we make up about them. However, I will also invite you to take a closer look at the confirmation bias we all have in selecting some Facts over others.

A quick reminder: Recall your previously identified "Big Challenge" and keep it in mind as you read this section.

The Three Sub-Directions of Facts

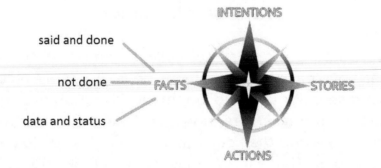

"Just the facts, ma'am."
"Well, which kind?"
Yes, you guessed it, the Facts Direction, like Intentions

and Actions, is divided into three sub directions: said & done, not done, and data & status. Using these sub directions will help you identify Facts that you may not otherwise notice.

<u>Said & Done</u>

The first step in separating Facts from Stories is to work out what was *actually* said and what was *actually* done. Ask yourself: Did I see it happen? Did I hear it happen? Or did I just hear from someone else that it happened?

Witnessing something firsthand gives you factual information, whereas hearing about it afterwards means that the information may be riddled with Stories. The Facts you obtain secondhand will always pertain more to the teller's telling of the event than to the event itself.

Let's revisit Geneva spilling her coffee. If I saw Geneva spill her coffee, then the Fact is:

Done: Geneva spilled her coffee.

However, if I did not observe Geneva spill her coffee, but she told me she had, the Fact is:

Said: Geneva told me she spilled her coffee.

While coffee spilling may not have serious repercussions in the grand scheme of things, relying on information you've been told is risky. Facts can be easily distorted as they move from person to person, just as the message is distorted in the grade school game of Telephone. It is always better to work with first-hand Facts, as doing so reduces the risk of distortion. The key to said & done is making sure you're clear about what information falls into what category, and not confusing the Facts of what you directly experienced as "said & done" with the alleged Facts buried in what someone else "said."

Finally, when focusing on Facts, try to be the video recorder and stay alert to your own filters and biases.

Now let's see how Deck and Matilda put together their said & done material.

DECK

Deck had always considered himself a man of Action and a man of Facts, but in his work with the Clarity Compass, he was beginning to realize he hadn't always known why he'd held certain Facts to be absolutely true, and others (usually the "Facts" others spouted) as bologna. He began by writing out a few relevant said & done Facts:

- *I conduct exit interviews.*
- *A couple of employees said to me as they were leaving, "You are overbearing." Or, "You yell at employees."*
- *Most of my female employees have cried during one-on-ones with me and a couple of the male employees have teared up.*

Deck shared with me that he has high standards and expects people to meet them. Surely it wasn't his fault when they fell short, right? But looking at this list of what was actually said and done, Deck found himself seeing that perhaps his disappointment had more to do with him than with them. He'd never thought of himself as the sort of man who would repeatedly make people cry, and was growing steadily less comfortable with the way his team members were reacting to his disappointment.

MATILDA

Matilda didn't typically hold a grudge, but at work she had been taking more mental notes than usual, partly out of fear after having been chided so much recently about her "oversight of details." Her said & done Facts list looked like this:

- **Ling assigns me eight to ten new projects each quarter.**
- **I have other projects that I clock more time into than Ling's projects.**
- **Ling said, "You're not being strategic in your projects."**
- **Ling said, "You are not extending your business and you are not drawing new business to the firm. This is critical to your success."**

Matilda had spent so long convincing herself that the problem was "Ling just doesn't listen to me" (her "said" to her friends) that she'd completely overlooked the specific direction he'd given her regarding being strategic (his "said"). Her scope and problem statement had always revolved around the seemingly biased reviews she was getting from Ling, which resulted in her dismissing the parts about strategy and totally failing to acknowledge her own culpability in the situation.

By writing out just a few Fact-based sentences, Matilda shifted her scope from trying to get good reviews to changing the way she approached strategic thinking. She still wanted to get better reviews and become a senior partner, but by writing out the Facts of the situation, she was able to name a clearly defined situational want: "I want to be acknowledged for being strategic at work." This was something she had some control over. She thought about starting over with a new Clarity Compass, but for time's sake, rewrote the scope of her current Clarity Compass to **"I want to be more strategic."**

Said & Done Case Study Wrap Up: Note the interesting reactions that arose after Deck and Matilda wrote down their said & done and reviewed the facts. Matilda rewrote her scope and Deck realized he made people cry. Also note that even as Deck and Matilda worked on their Facts, their reactions to and interpretations of them are still Stories.

Practicing Said & Done

To practice said & done, think of the last interaction you had. Paint the big picture: Where were you and who were you with? What was going on in the background? What events or conversations can you recall that might have led up to or foreshadowed the interaction? Once you've noted the data within the scene, work through the following steps:

1. Jot down some of the things you heard said or saw done.
2. Double check to make sure you have only written down things that a video camera would capture directly. Cut any items that do not meet this criterion.
3. Let's try another example. Reflect on the last heated exchange you had.
4. Jot down some of the things that you heard said or saw done, by yourself or the Other.

5. What do you observe in this situation through the lens of a video camera?
6. Notice where it might've been more difficult for you to keep Stories out of your writing because it was a heated exchange.

Not Done

In addition to getting clear about what is said & done in any given situation, we also have to define what is *not* done. Specifically, in this sub direction, we're focusing on and comparing what we expected of a situation to how it played out—what aligned, what did not?

Note that neither our expectations nor our hopes are Facts. However, the absence of physical Action related to our expectations or hopes is a Fact. It is often the case that the reason we're upset or disappointed is rooted in what a person did not do (Fact) in relation to what we expected them to do (Story).

To return to the coffee-spilling example, I might generate the following not done list:

Fact: No one helped Geneva clean up the coffee.

Fact: Frank was standing next to Geneva and did not help her clean up.

Again, be wary of Stories that sneak their way into your not done, like the ones below:

Story: Frank should have helped Geneva clean up.

The not done was that Frank did not help Geneva. The observer who said, "Frank should have helped Geneva clean up," created a story by including an expectation or hope about Frank's behavior. As soon as we add the "should have," a judgment is made and the sentence becomes a Story instead of a Fact.

Making a clean distinction between Facts and Stories is, of course, often very tricky because even the words used to describe a Fact can relay an implicit Story. For example, it's a Fact that Frank was standing "right" next to Geneva. But we could also say, "Frank was standing next to Geneva." Some people might include the word "right" in the sentence, (i.e. "Frank was standing right next to Geneva") as a way to imply that "he was available to help her," which is a Story. Including the word "right" does not automatically make the sentence a Story. However, when you're trying to deescalate an interpersonal conflict, it is best to keep the distinction between Facts and Stories as clean as possible, and to avoid allowing potentially leading or inflammatory language to appear in the Facts section.

Now let's see how Deck and Matilda documented the not done sub direction.

DECK

Deck combed through his email exchanges with the last employee who left, and wrote down dozens of examples of how this person had not lived up to his expectations, or had not done what he'd asked. Browsing through emails he had exchanged with other employees, he discovered more of the same issues, and automatically started to feel annoyed with the way people had failed him. "Just look at all they had not done!"

But then Deck paused. He considered the possibility that he might be focusing too much on what his employees didn't do, which could ultimately only continue to prove to him that they were wrong and incompetent. He was starting to sense that this many people couldn't be wrong and incompetent this regularly. Maybe there were not done activities he could observe that did not contribute to his story of their incompetence. He noted in his not done list:

- *Most of my employees don't ask for references before they leave.*
- *Most employees only give me positive feedback when they leave, and rarely if ever mention anything negative.*
- *Any positive feedback about me is about being smart, hard-working, or successful, but never mentions them enjoying working with me or me being good boss.*
- *Most employees leave without giving more than a weeks' notice and some leave with no notice.*

By reviewing what employees did after they were already out the door, Deck realized, "I haven't given the issue this level of thought before now. I figured employees didn't know how good they had it here, found something they believed was better, and moved on." But the longer he sat with the words in front of him, the more he realized that such large numbers of people don't just "find something better." There was a reason people were leaving. For the first time, Deck entertained the idea that the great exodus of hard-working, smart people might be because of him.

MATILDA

Matilda was already quite familiar with not done's from her swimming career. In the early years, Matilda had not put enough hours into her swimming practice. The consequence of this not done was that she didn't meet the expectations of her parents, her coach, and especially herself. Consequently, she cramped up, lost races, and almost dropped out of competitive swimming.

The not done exercise came naturally to her, especially since she had changed her scope to focus on improving her strategic thinking. Her list included:

- *I haven't included a strategy section in my project proposals.*
- *I haven't brought in any new business this year.*
- *I haven't made any attempt to forge any new vendor alliances this year.*

Now that Matilda had gotten honest with herself, and as a result, the ways she hadn't lived up to her own expectations of being a high performer came sharply into focus and she knew where she needed and wanted to improve. Though she felt slightly ashamed of her shortcomings, she could see a path to success clearly laid out in front of her.

Not Done Case Study Wrap Up: Note the interesting and very different realizations Deck and Matilda triggered by deeply exploring their not done sub direction. It was a huge (and semi-painful) realization for Deck that he might be part of the problem and a huge (and positive) step for Matilda to see a path towards success.

Practicing Not Done

For this activity, reflect a bit first on all the times in the last few weeks where someone has disappointed you.

Were you hoping for a relaxing getaway weekend in the sun with your spouse, but instead you spent two days doing yard work because they missed a big deadline and needed to work on Saturday? Did that report arrive a half a day too late because your colleague simply assumed "End of Day" meant midnight, and not 5:00 p.m.? Pull out a piece of paper and a pen, and then:

1. List briefly what happened.
2. Make note in each case where a **not done** took place, meaning there was something you had anticipated someone would do, and they didn't do it.
3. Write down the **expectation** you had of the other person that they did not meet. Sometimes this exercise is as simple as stating, "I expected the person to X." It may seem like an oversimplification, but writing out these unmet expectations helps to separate the Story from the Facts. Fact: Somebody didn't do X. Story: I believe they should have done X. Or Story: Whether they should have or not, I expected them to do X.

Data & Status

One of the best tools for separating Facts from Stories is quantifying the "hard" data and status related to a given situation. When I talk about data & status, I'm talking about numbers, titles, and labels. Numbers, for example, are things like profit totals, the number of lost production days due to illness or injury, the number of deliveries or phone calls, and the number of years or hours worked on a project or in a position. Status would be things like an individual's title as director, individual contributor, or manager. Data & status consists of all the stuff we can see right there on paper—in reports, emails, or on our office door.

In my own life and in working with my clients, I've found it true time and time again that when we take the time to observe the data in any given situation, it often helps us cut through our subjective interpretations (Stories) and get down to the objective Facts. This can be a painful exercise sometimes, as the data may reveal a picture that contradicts our own Stories, revealing Blind Spots in our Reality Maps. This is why people tend to avoid this exercise like the plague. But when done with a sincere desire to transform, this exercise never fails to yield positive results.

While working through your data & status, it's important to note that the emphasis should not be on the exact precision of any numbers, but on the best approximation of numbers that are useful. Be pragmatic.

Now, to get a better sense of how data & status can turn challenging situations around, let's return to Deck and Matilda.

DECK

As soon as Deck began to compile his data & status list, his heart sank. How could he show such patience and generosity with his kids and two four-legged beasts at home, but show nothing but disappointment and outrage with so many employees? His rough tallies were enough to paint a clear picture.

- ***I've used a term or phrase that expressed disappointment or annoyance at an employee via*** *email one hundred and forty times in the last year.*

- *I've received two hundred apology emails in the last year, since some people apologized preemptively.*
- *I pay my employees at twenty-two percent above-average industry rates.*
- *They leave after an average of thirteen months.*

As Deck sat with this data, his frustration at his employees subsided, while the cumulative weight of so many employee apologies felt staggering. It hit him: I haven't given people enough time to fulfill my expectations.

Opening up to this one cold, hard truth, Deck then began to take note of how often he had expressed anger in those same emails: sixty-five angry emails! That was a lot of anger. Deck was overwhelmed by how poorly he had behaved towards his employees, and began to contemplate the even tougher question: Where was all that anger coming from? If he could answer that, he could transform his Reality Maps, his life, and the lives of so many others.

MATILDA

Matilda had been a numbers person as a swimmer. She knew the difference half of a centimeter or half a second made. What kind of fractions or numbers were keeping her from where she wanted to be? Still, when it came to using her acumen for numbers in this exercise, she was originally hesitant: Wouldn't this possibly distract her from her new focus on strategy? But she trusted in the

Clarity Compass now, appreciated the structure of each practice, and stepped up to the plate.

- *My numeric rating for "overall performance" reviews is in the top ten percent for junior partners across the firm.*
- *While I meet other requirements, the rating is not within the top seven percent required by policy for becoming senior partner.*
- *Seven emails sent from Ling describing a strategy that he'd come up with.*
- *Ten proposals were created without strategy sections*
- *Two accepted invitations to conferences this year.*
- *Five declined conference invitations this year.*

Matilda saw a lot of low-hanging fruit in these numbers. Counting up the opportunities she had ignored further validated Ling's point. The data verified—and this is perhaps one reason so many clients of mine are intuitively reluctant to working through this particular exercise—that for too long, she hadn't been concerning herself enough with strategy. It made the path that had begun to appear before her in the previous practice appear even straighter.

Data & Status Case Study Wrap Up: Note how Deck was initially overwhelmed by what he learned from the data and Matilda was encouraged and reinforced by it—demonstrating that the particular emotional reaction we have to any of the sub directions is not as critical as whether or not that sub direction helps deepen our understanding of the situation and ourselves.

Practicing Data & Status

Data & status can help support arguments we have already put forth, but they can also reveal our Blind Spots. And while we are generally all already swamped with too much information, it is important to invest the time in exploring the data that is relevant in our own Clarity Compass situations. The intention behind this exercise is to figure out where including data is most helpful. We want to look at the kinds of information we are providing, and become more aware of where we could more strategically place dollar amounts, dates, or statistics.

1. Review the last ten emails you've sent.
2. Note within each email where you have cited data, updated others on the specific status of a project, or in general provided numbers, dates, or statistics.
3. Approach the next ten emails you send them with increased awareness of where and how you are including particular pieces of data & status. Where are you providing data that recipients aren't interested in? What data are you not providing that they might want or need to see?

Confirmation Bias

The Facts Direction serves two primary purposes: to invite us to be more grounded in Facts as a basis for thinking and conversing, and to realize our biases in selecting the Facts that we pick. Once we learn to distinguish Facts from Stories, there's a temptation to assume we've mastered objectivity. Don't be fooled. The way we frame the Facts we've collected can still be distorted in support of our Stories. At the end of the day, you, the observer, will always be choosing which Facts to focus on and which to ignore or deemphasize. And that's where cognitive bias comes in.

Cognitive bias is a complex and exciting field of study that explores the many ways in which the Blind Spots in our Reality Maps are formed. You might even think of it as the psychology of Blind Spots. One particular type of cognitive bias, the confirmation bias, is basically skewed fact-picking, or our tendency to seek out those things that confirm what we already believe.

Our senses deliver an infinite number of observations, so why do we choose any one particular thing that was said or done over all the others? While the Facts that we select are our direct observations, we make those selections because of our Stories. Stories will always be with us, but if we can push ourselves a bit to avoid trusting those Stories *implicitly*, we can go further in grounding ourselves in physical reality. Remember, total objective reality is not something we can achieve, but observing physical reality gets us closer to the objective. To illustrate this concept, let me introduce you to my friends, Tony and Jenna.

Tony and Jenna have been dating happily for two years. In general, Tony knew Jenna to be a very loving partner—someone who would go out of her way to listen to, care for, and support him. And then *The Argument* happened. One night, Tony came off a frustrating phone call with his best friend, Diego. Tony relayed the conversation to Jenna as they sat down to dinner, and each time he expressed pain regarding some aspect of the phone call, Jenna replied with a comment that supported Diego's perspective. She repeatedly encouraged Tony to step into Diego's shoes, without expressing any sympathy for Tony. After about fifteen minutes, Tony fell silent and changed the subject. "Wow, Jenna's not a very loving and supportive partner," he thought.

He began to think of other times where she cut him off in conversation, had ignored something that was important to him, or where she had just been looking out for herself. Based on the Facts he had selected in the moment, it seemed true that Jenna was not a loving and supportive partner. His criteria for selecting the Facts were skewed by how she was currently behaving in an interaction where he acutely wanted her support. What Tony wasn't seeing in that moment was how the narrow set of Facts he'd deemed relevant was skewing his perception. He'd drawn a sweeping conclusion about Jenna from a fifteen-minute interaction, which couldn't possibly provide enough context to see Jenna's actual role in their relationship. He was ignoring the larger picture and looking at specific data—all somewhat emotionally charged—that supported his current short-term conclusion. Yet if he had forced himself to look at a broader set of Facts—say, the way Jenna had dropped whatever she was doing almost every time Tony had been upset about something over the past two years—then he would see that Jenna indeed was a very loving and supportive partner over time.

We've all had an experience similar to Tony's, where a single, heated conversation swayed our opinion about someone and caused us to react (or overreact) in that moment. How often do we base our evaluations of someone on one isolated experience and fail to see the bigger picture? Try to always broaden the Stories that influence which Facts you keep in mind.

When we work with Facts, the first step is to focus on observations rather than Stories and opinions. The next step is to reevaluate the criteria with which we select our Facts. And since the Facts we examine usually build toward a case or Story, the third step is to stay open and curious to the Facts that other people present.

<u>Practicing the Facts Direction</u>

Writing Practice: As preparation for your practice, review what you've written out on your "Big Challenge" for your said & done, not done, and data & status.

Next, think of a new situation and bring to mind the video camera I've been referring to throughout this book. Take some time moving the camera lens in and out on the situation—panning out for the big picture and zooming in for the close-up. Once you've got a scene "playing out," do the following:

1. Mentally ask yourself, "Is this what a video camera would record?"
2. In your day-to-day conversations, practice stating the Facts you think are key to the conversation. Using your own language, encourage your conversation partner to also name the Facts they see as key.
3. Write out a few sentences about this situation, clearly defining the things said & done, not done, and data & status. As you read through your list, do you have any new insights?

The Stories Direction

In the last section, we looked at how establishing the objective Facts of a situation can give you a sturdier foundation on which to base your decisions. We also explored how easy it is to confuse our Stories for Facts and how often we tend to distort the selection of Facts in ways that lead us astray. But I don't want to imply that Stories are the enemy. Stories play a pivotal role in creating meaning around the Facts we collect, the Intentions we pursue, and the Actions we take. In fact, the Stories Direction is what we use to navigate our own Reality Maps.

Our Stories, both grand and specific, organize and make meaning of the Facts from which our Reality Maps are made. We rely on them to navigate our experiences. They help us make sense of an otherwise complex and chaotic world. Stories, unlike Facts, are inherently subjective. They represent our opinions, ideas, conclusions, visceral responses, and emotional reactions to the world as we experience it.

By examining our Stories, we are able to take responsibility for the Reality Maps that influence our experience of life and behavior while finding areas in which we can meaningfully change. But change is a difficult task, in part, because of the Ego.

Taming the Ego

Given the prevalence and power of social media, we have probably never been more aware of how many people think differently than we do. Our friends, family, and colleagues are all willing to argue for their own correctness—as are we. At times, we realize the futility of pressing others to adopt our Stories, our ideas, beliefs, and opinions. But more often than not, our Egos entice us into believing our Stories are right without our being aware we're making this assumption.

If we want to see more clearly, it's crucial that we keep a steady and continual eye on our Ego. We need to keep the Ego in check if we want to understand just how much it affects our choices and distorts our worldview. As we awaken to our Ego, we start to see how much we have been ruled by its primitive knee-jerk impulse to control, to be right, and to adamantly protect our Stories at all costs.

So, the first step in seeing through our Ego's mechanisms—after we've acknowledged its power—is to step back from it and ask: *Why am I so sure that I'm right, and so many other people are wrong?* This question can terrify the Ego because it goes against everything it has built over a lifetime. But if we can push through our existential fears, deliberately questioning our "rightness" and looking courageously at the cracks in our Reality Maps, we can create a space for making wiser, more effective choices.

The need to be right doesn't always look like someone busting a neck vein, turning red in the face, and pointing a finger. Being right is more about the many subtle behaviors and assumptions (most of which we are totally unaware of) that come together to form our perspective. The Clarity Compass helps us to discern between our *stated beliefs*—the beliefs that we tell ourselves and others—and our *demonstrated beliefs*—those that can be determined by observing our behaviors. From our own limited perspectives, our stated and demonstrated beliefs often appear to be the same. Why wouldn't they? But the inconsistencies between what we state and what we demonstrate are usually much more apparent to other people. The goal of the Clarity Compass is to shrink the gap between what we *say* and what we *do*.

Of course, the Ego is not all bad—it performs a vital function in our lives. Sure, it may at times be a power-hungry tyrant defending its power base, but underneath the façade, it is an over-worked technician trying its best to maintain control in order to keep everyone feeling safe and certain in an ambiguous world. So while it's crucial to see the ugliness of your Ego, it's also important to empathize with it. Cultivate some levity and curiosity as you explore the ways in which your Ego grips and controls you and others. Then begin to let go. Free yourself of judgment and be gentle in the way you approach your impulses.

Be patient, yet unwavering in your exploration. Give your Ego the time it needs to adjust from serving itself to serving your Heart. Where your Ego finds meaning in control, your Heart finds meaning in connection, in building relationships with yourself and others, and aligning it all with true purpose. As you begin to tame your Ego, it begins to soften to your Heart's lead, and your life falls into a more harmonious state of wellbeing and success.

I've worked with dozens of powerful, intelligent leaders over the years who have told me that the Clarity Compass forced them to acknowledge their unconscious beliefs and the ways in which their long-held positions were off. Many of them had received nothing but positive feedback over the years about how engaging, brilliant, charismatic, or friendly they were. This is all well and good—we thrive on positive feedback, of course— but after receiving so much of it, they naturally begin to develop Blind Spots. They couldn't imagine ways in which their interpersonal engagement might benefit from a shift in perspective, because like many people, they found it easier to continue doing what they had been doing. "Why fix it if it ain't broke?"

The problem with this mentality is that it can lead to stagnation and holding patterns. It can result in lost opportunities, which are missed in part because of a total lack of awareness they exist in the first place. When these leaders I worked with began to see how damaging some of their actions, inactions, and interactions had been, they often retreated—at first—back into denial. It is preferable to feeling the shame of not being as skilled, helpful, or appropriate as they thought they were. However, confronting the truth helped propel them toward more successful relationships at work and at home and led them to greater fulfillment.

It is never too late to dig below the accolades and purely positive feedback we all crave in order to face tougher truths and shift our perspective. Anyone with even a smidgen of self-awareness has probably had an experience where they were arguing vehemently, only to realize mid-sentence that they were wrong. Often times, the Ego kicks in at this point and feels too ashamed to admit its errors. Remember, it typically strives to mitigate damage, keep control and save face. Similarly, as we begin to wake up to how long and how far we've been led by our Egos, we can sometimes feel ashamed. Shame is a natural resistance to acknowledging our unconscious beliefs, and experiencing it is a reminder to stay on your course. Shame, in fact, may be an indicator that you're on the right path and headed toward real growth. So don't beat yourself down. You are here for awakening, not punishment. On the other side of shame lies radical clarity and opportunity.

This "other side" I'm talking about shouldn't be confused with some sort of nirvana. Just as there is no way of achieving one hundred percent objectivity, there is no final and perfect understanding of reality. No matter how many new perspectives we consider and honor, we will always be operating from a limited field of view. As we conquer some of the biases caused by our Blind Spots, new ones will push to the surface. The primary goal of examining our Stories is not to judge or feel ashamed of them, but to awaken to our ingrained ways of thinking— to reevaluate and decide which Stories we want to keep and which we desire to change, in order to expand and grow our Reality Maps.

Once again, here is your quick reminder: Bring to mind your previously identified "Big Challenge" and keep it there as you continue with these pages.

The Three Sub Directions of Stories

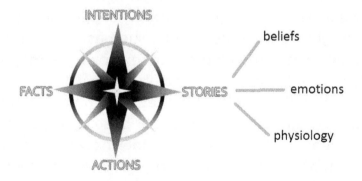

The three components or sub directions for Stories are beliefs, emotions, and physiology. Each represents a fundamental aspect of the internal world of any character

DR. BRIT POULSON

in a story. Think about the characters in the novels that you read. They hold to an inner dialogue based on what they believe is happening. They react emotionally to what they believe is happening. Ultimately, these beliefs and emotions often lead to some kind of physical reaction. By exploring these three sub directions, we'll be better able to sort through our subjective inner world, reducing inner chaos and inspiring us to examine aspects of our internal experience that have thus far remained hidden. As we sort through our beliefs, emotions, and physiology, we can make different choices about the character that we are playing in our own lives—and we can choose to alter our role.

Beliefs

Our Stories manifest, in part, through our beliefs, and they affect the way we navigate the world. Our beliefs range from conscious to unconscious, beneficial to harmful, stated to demonstrated, broad to specific, and superficial to deep-rooted. They might be political beliefs, such as the party you generally support in elections. They might be spiritual beliefs, such as whether or not you believe in some kind of higher power. Some beliefs are less "A or B, yes or no" and are more values-oriented, such as whether you believe that human beings are fundamentally altruistic and good, or base and self-serving. As you read, I invite you to consider how many types of beliefs might be showing up in your internal experience and affecting the way you navigate the world.

In our attempt to become conscious of our own beliefs and how they manifest in our lives, it's helpful to understand the various types of beliefs we have.

104

Throughout this text we've already implicitly discussed conscious versus unconscious beliefs, as well as beliefs that are harmful versus helpful. In the Taming the Ego section, we discussed stated versus demonstrated beliefs. Now let's look further into broad versus specific beliefs and superficial versus deep-rooted beliefs:

Broad versus Specific Beliefs:

Some beliefs can be considered global or universal. For example: People are honest; corporations are greedy; and corporations will take care of their employees. I've seen people hold these beliefs—which I call broad beliefs—as if they were true, regardless of particular situations or experiences that might change their stance, or regardless of how much conflicting information they encounter. They tend to be based on trends we assume across entire categories of experience.

Other beliefs are related to specific entities, experiences, or individuals. If someone is holding a belief that is situational, the belief should ideally pertain only to the situation. A person could say, "I believe that executive A knows what she is doing, but executive B does not." Or "I believe that company A doesn't treat its employees well. Company B does." And so on. I invite you to begin to examine what beliefs you hold for particular situations versus what beliefs you hold across a wide variety of experiences.

Superficial versus Deep-Rooted Beliefs

This distinction points out the difference between how lightly we hold a belief versus how deeply ingrained it is in our Reality Maps.

Any of the beliefs that we would hold onto, even in the face of a fair amount of "contrary" evidence, are deeply rooted beliefs. How much evidence we would need to change our minds determines just how deeply seated they are. That said, these questions don't help us to determine if a particular belief is helpful or not. Nor do they necessarily guide us in how to let any belief go. They simply help us to recognize how attached we are to our belief. You can get to the root of this distinction by asking:

1. What are the beliefs (opinions and assumptions) that I have in this situation?
2. For each of these beliefs and assumptions, if I had a fair amount of evidence to the contrary, which would I have difficulty letting go of?

For example, say a person believes that all corporations are bad because they abuse employees. If they encounter solid evidence that a handful of corporations are good to their employees and communities, and yet they still hold onto their initial belief, the belief is deep-seated. If they change their belief about corporations being bad and acknowledge that some corporations are good based only on a few encounters, then the belief is more superficial.

Similarly, with specific beliefs, if I believe an executive, Patsy, doesn't know what she is doing, but I then experience many occasions where the she makes competent decisions and I refuse to change my specific belief about Patsy, this belief is deep-rooted. But if I easily shift my opinion of Patsy to acknowledge that she has some competence, the belief is superficial.

The intention of the superficial versus deep-rooted distinction is to become aware of how tightly we hold some of our beliefs.

In the end, if we have beliefs that are broad, we need to be wary of where we encounter exceptions. Where our beliefs are deep-rooted, we need to be careful of how we are clinging to them so adamantly that we are doing ourselves and others a disservice. Similarly, if we have beliefs that are too specific, we might miss important trends. And, if our beliefs switch too readily, we may find that we lack tenacity and character in moving forward important initiatives.

Imagining Better Beliefs and Dispositions

As we've been discussing, our beliefs shape our reality, for better or for worse. When we uncover our beliefs, we often discover ways in which they have been distorting our Reality Maps. Since our belief systems form the foundational structure of our Reality Maps, a key initiative in renovating your Reality Maps is adopting new beliefs and dispositions. Primarily, I want the Clarity Compass to support you in exploring your belief systems in a way that invites you to imagine new and more helpful ways of thinking about specific situations and your life. You consciously decide what is best for you to believe.

Many people have asked me to suggest some specific foundational beliefs, dispositions, or root metaphors that are helpful. While this book is not focused on being prescriptive about particular beliefs that are better than others, an easy example of a great one is gratitude, or believing that you are fortunate or lucky. There is much research that demonstrates that having a disposition of gratitude is critical in terms of attaining personal health, great relationships, and the pursuit of happiness. Using gratitude as an example, I invite you to think through, "What beliefs do I want to consciously cultivate within myself?"

Now let's return to our case studies and see how Deck and Matilda explored their beliefs.

DECK

Deck checked internally for the beliefs that were influencing his situation. ***What beliefs am I holding, particularly around interacting with my employees that might be affecting my behavior?*** Keep in mind that Deck has subtly shifted his scope sub direction from retaining his employees to improving his interactions with them. This doesn't mean he's given up entirely on retaining his employees, but that he's found a specific issue embedded within the larger problem, and has moved toward this invitation to revise a more narrowly focused Clarity Compass.

Deck sat for a moment, staring at the photos of his kids and dogs and then wrote down his principal belief about employees:

> ***Since I'm paying for their labor, I deserve to get what I pay for.***

Looking again at the photos on his desk and taking a very deep breath, Deck suddenly realized how tightly he had been holding onto this belief. He also saw how his anger was linked to it. Since he was paying his employees above industry standards, he felt entitled to certain "benefits." Namely, he felt he shouldn't ever be questioned about the demands he made. As he started to see his belief was just another subjective experience, a second thought came: **Nobody cares about what I deserve.** While this deeper realization felt horribly, devastatingly true, it also felt freeing.

Going through this process felt like a confession for Deck—he named a secret fear he'd hidden from himself for years:

- *I'm afraid no one cares about me. I'm afraid that I'm unimportant and if I'm not demanding and doling out incentives, no one will do anything for me.*

Further thoughts rose to the surface:

- *They don't care about what I think I deserve. They have their own lives to live.*

And finally:

- *They don't care about what I think I deserve because of the way I treat them.*

Deck was unearthing old, deep-seated, and broad beliefs that he knew linked to—and influenced—all sorts of interactions throughout his life, including financially fueled ones. As he continued writing out his beliefs, he moved from deep-seated and interior beliefs to new beliefs that were arising even as he was processing them, such as the belief that employees don't care about him because of the way he treated them. Strangely, instead of feeling overtaken by these realizations, Deck felt humbled and grateful. It was clear to him that these beliefs were having a significant impact on how he was behaving towards his employees, and in acknowledging them, he started to feel hopeful. Once hope enters the picture, trust me, things begin to turn.

MATILDA

Matilda too, prepped to take a more thoughtful look at how her beliefs were standing in the way of what she wanted. She wrote:

- *I work hard*
- *I have good ideas.*

It was a decent start, but thanks to the work she had already done with the Clarity Compass, Matilda was beginning to acquire the sense to know when she wasn't digging deep enough. So, she kept digging:

- *I have always been a hard worker.*
- *I've had good ideas from the beginning.*

And then she continued, somewhat afraid, but mostly inspired by the rush that uncovering deeply held beliefs brings about:

- *I've been so buried in inconsequential garbage that I have forgotten to value my own ideas.*
- *Ling gives me too much busywork. He's stifling my productivity.*

Matilda read these beliefs back and was startled by the level of animosity she'd held for Ling. She decided to let her newfound emphasis on the strategy problem rest for the moment. The problem with Ling needed her immediate attention.

Beliefs Case Study Wrap Up: Note how many levels of digging into their beliefs Deck and Matilda went through in order to reach new understandings of themselves and others. Then note how Deck experienced a range of feelings, ending with one of hope. Note how Matilda was startled by the depth of animosity she had uncovered. This level of discovery is to be expected when digging deep inside one's belief systems.

A Note about Changing Scope

"We can't solve our problems with the same level of thinking we used to create them." Variations of this quote are attributed to Einstein, and I believe it speaks to the heart of what the Clarity Compass is all about. In fact, one of the primary results of working with the Clarity Compass is that your thinking will actually shift to a higher level. When this happens, it's often the case that the original definition of the problem you're working on shifts and morphs. The problem statement that you placed in your original scope needs to be adjusted since you have evolved beyond the level of thinking that created the problem.

The success of your Clarity Compass often depends on your willingness to go back and refine your original scope. Doing this is crucial because it will facilitate you in coming up with a better solution. Realizing that you need to alter your scope can occur within any sub direction of the Clarity Compass. For Matilda, this realization occurred within her beliefs sub direction. In Matilda's case, she has been maintaining multiple scopes in one Clarity Compass. Recall:

Scope 1: Getting good reviews.
Scope 2: Ling refusing to acknowledge her good work.
Scope 3: Becoming more strategic.
Scope 4: Ling prevents her from being productive through busywork.

The latter three scopes are clearly embedded within the larger first scope because they all impact receiving good reviews. Even though Matilda is including sub scopes in her larger scope, her Clarity Compass is helpful, but see where she jumps back and forth with her need to be more strategic versus her contentious relationship with Ling? If you have the time and the energy, it usually pays off to quickly think through the Clarity Compass for any sub scopes or problem statements that arise in the middle of another Clarity Compass. Explore which embedded scopes or problem statements warrant more in-depth investigation in a separate Clarity Compass rather than cluttering many problems in one Clarity Compass exploration.

These case studies are only a portion of all of the different Stories Deck and Matilda examined—they also represent a mere drop in the bucket in regards to the plethora of beliefs, assumptions, world views, schemas, concepts, thoughts, and cognitions that we can examine in our own lives.

Practicing Beliefs

The key to practicing this sub direction is waking up to the broad and specific beliefs that undergird our thoughts, feelings, and Actions—and then owning our level of attachment to those beliefs.

Think of a few recent disagreements. They don't have to be heated or significantly conflicted, but bring to mind times you experienced some point of contention or difference in terms of how you approached or solved a particular situation. Then:

1. Make a list of the positions that the other person (or persons) in this disagreement took.
2. With each of the positions they took, note:
   a. Where you gave counter information to discount their belief.
   b. How strongly you disagreed and believed that your position was correct.
   c. Where your assertion was based on Facts and where your assertion was more opinion-based.
   d. Where you find yourself uncomfortable in acknowledging that some portion of your stance was primarily opinion-based.

Remember to fear not. Finding that you hold some beliefs a bit too fiercely only makes you human and provides an opportunity to loosen your tight grip on Reality Maps.

Emotions

Emotions serve a variety of functions, guiding everything from basic everyday communications to expressing the depths of our soul. Our emotions help us survive and thrive: Our fear helps us avoid sketchy alleys or moves us out of the way of speeding car; our anger helps us stand up for ourselves when we have a righteous cause; our sadness allows us to work through grief; and our joy moves us to appreciate living.

Sometimes emotions are difficult to identify particularly when we have so many different words to describe similar emotions. To make it easier to access and identify our emotions when we are feeling distracted, confused, or rushed, it's helpful to realize that most of our emotions are derivations of some combination of the four primary emotions: sad, mad, glad, and afraid. Often, it's easier to reference a primary emotion and call it a day. Other times, it's important to find a more nuanced name for the emotions we are experiencing.

Many people consider emotions to be synonymous with feelings, but for Clarity Compass purposes, feelings can encompass all of our felt senses. These include emotions, chaotic intuitive beliefs, and somatic experiences. We'll explore the latter further in the next sub direction, physiology.

Emotions and feelings fall under the Stories direction because of the instrumental role they play in our subjective experience. They influence our biases, judgments, and predispositions. Emotions help to solidify our beliefs, and our beliefs, in turn, generate a wide range of emotions. It is often our emotional attachment to our beliefs that makes it difficult to consider other perspectives and investigate our Blind Spots objectively. When you identify your emotions and feelings, and look critically at your beliefs, you begin to break the cycle of living by only one Reality Map, and you imagine better Stories to live by.

When I invite clients to write down their emotions and feelings regarding a situation, I am no longer surprised at how many of them initially feel they are becoming crazier.

"Stay on the course," I say. "Hold onto that Clarity Compass."

The process of honestly writing it all out makes us saner. Naming our emotions and feelings distances us from them—doesn't that sound like a relief? As our unconscious drives are brought to light, we gain the opportunity for greater self-assessment, self-awareness, and self-management. When we acknowledge our emotions and feelings, we can harness them and operate more powerfully. Rather than obstacles that continually cause us to stumble or freeze, they become fuel for energetic <u>motion</u>, or e-motion—and onward we march.

Now let's return to Deck and Matilda and see how they confronted the emotions surrounding their situations.

DECK

The Clarity Compass forced Deck to confront some heavy, deeply buried emotions and feelings. As you can imagine, this was no walk in the dog park for him. Deck had been running from his emotions for years, and as a result they had begun to run him. But he was beginning to feel the loosening of the shackles he'd been bound by for so long. So he stuck it out and continued to look for any other feelings or emotions regarding his situation.

The most immediate feeling he noticed was a sense of being out of control. He didn't express this feeling in a conscious thought (he never said to me, "I'm out of control, Brit!"), but he mentioned a vague sense of chaos around him that he could not easily manage. The emotion he associated with this chaos was **fear**.

Another emotion he acknowledged was **loneliness** in the form of weakness and overwhelming need, which was accompanied by shortness of breath. He wrote that down, checking in with himself again. Now he could identify a low-level **shame** bubbling inside him, as well as a mixture of self-pity and **anxiety**. His completed list was heavy: *Fear, loneliness, shame, anxiety*. While he was excruciatingly uncomfortable with all these emotions, he was also confident that relief would eventually come just by acknowledging and articulating what he was feeling.

MATILDA

Matilda looked over her list of Facts and beliefs, keeping a particular eye out for anything involving Ling.

- *I am really <u>worked up</u> about Ling stifling my abilities.*
- *I am <u>resentful</u> that he's prevented me from producing my best work.*
- *I am <u>sad</u> that I've wasted so much time trying to appease someone who is actively keeping me down.*

Matilda's emotions and feelings are **worked up, resentful, and sad**. The remaining content in each sentence are beliefs. It's fine to write up the emotions this way, as long as the distinction between emotions and beliefs is made. Matilda felt tired, but calmer and quieter than she had in a while. Acknowledging the strength of her emotions provided her with a clearer picture of how they were affecting her disposition and behavior.

Emotions Case Study Wrap Up: Dealing with very powerful emotions, both Deck and Matilda were left feeling confronted, drained, and a bit raw. At the same time, both clients admitted to a renewed sense of confidence and hope after completing the exercise.

Practicing Emotions

The first trick in acknowledging our emotions is taking the time to notice the obvious ones. The second trick is to become more aware of the ones we are in tuned with, but that are still impacting us. Think of the last time you felt some emotion, then ask yourself the following questions:

1. If you were aware of any emotions in the moment, which ones did you predominantly experience?
2. At what point did you consciously reflect on that emotion rather than react to it or act on it?
3. Were there other secondary or subtler emotions that you can bring awareness to at this point?

The next time you're in the middle of an emotional experience, go through this exercise. Start with the predominant emotion and work your way toward subtler and subtler ones. For extra practice, you may even ask yourself if deeper wants are being satisfied, or not, and how they might be affecting your emotions.

Physiology

Modern lives are becoming more and more intellectual. Unless you work in a trade (and there are fewer of us who do), most of our work lives are dominated by technology, information, planning, analyzing, and coordinating. As a result, we've become more disconnected from our bodies. Except for injury or illness, and beyond weekly workouts, it's rare that we slow down enough to connect at a more profound level with our physicality. This disconnection is unfortunate and even dangerous, because research (and experience) shows that when we connect with our bodies, we can more easily begin to integrate our experiences and create better wellbeing.

Our bodies provide a powerful feedback mechanism for uncovering Blind Spots in our Reality Maps. We can use the physiology sub direction to search for clues that indicate a subjective experience is having a huge impact on our lives, even if it is less conscious, or less accessible to our conscious awareness. For example, I have worked with people who didn't know they were frustrated until they noticed themselves clenching their jaws, tapping a pencil, pacing, experiencing a constant low-grade stomachache or headache, or feeling flushed. These physical symptoms are often the result of some unresolved issues, and we need to recognize and flag them.

Think about the number of times have you made a choice based on intuition and things turned out well. The term "gut feeling" isn't just a figure of speech. Sometimes our bodies pick up on information that our conscious minds cannot process. These visceral responses are available 24/7. You only need to pay attention. Listen to your body's signals—let them do some of the legwork for you when making decisions and choosing one path or another.

Noticing how, when, and where you feel sensations in your body gives you clues about your subconscious and how it reacts to any number of situations. Your physiology may indicate that you need a break or that you should leave a conversation in order to avoid damaging a relationship. Noticing the manifestation of physical symptoms allows you to make self-care a priority. Your physiology can indicate that you need to come up with a new strategy. It may even prompt you to work through a second or third Clarity Compass.

So how do we bring into consciousness what we are carrying around unrecognized or unacknowledged? Sit still, close your eyes, take a deep breath—no, you don't have to be a Zen master to do any of this—and ask:

- Where is my body now?
- My mind?
- My Heart?
- How are all of these elements working together?
- Are they working together?

Sit quietly for a moment and let awareness spread through your body. Under what circumstances, do you tend to turn red, sweat, or feel sick to your stomach? When does your belly knot up? When do your hands start to shake?

Now focus on your "Big Challenge." How does your breathing feel? Where are you holding tension in your body?

Let's see how Deck and Matilda explored their physiology.

DECK

Deck had already connected a bit with his body when he'd looked at his emotions and feelings, so he was ready to take full stock. He had experienced a feeling of tension throughout his body and a shortness of breath associated with fear. He expressed a sinking feeling in his gut, tracked an uncomfortable stirring sensation in his chest, and felt a wave of heat rising up from his body and burning his face.

With such intense feelings and bodily sensations emerging just by putting his attention on employee turn-over rate, Deck realized that he was feeling a low-grade level of angst *all the time*. He worried about how much energy was being drained from his "emotional gas tank" daily, and then began to imagine what it would be like to live in an entirely different physical and emotional state. He stretched in his chair just thinking about how different his body, mind, and Heart might feel if he could transform his resentment, anger, and fear into passion and joy toward his work and his employees.

MATILDA

Matilda closed her eyes, took a few deep breaths, and started her body scan. Like Deck, she discovered her body was riddled with aches and pains and grievances.

- ***I feel a sharp pain between my eyebrows.***
- ***My shoulders feel achy and heavy.***
- ***Frequently, when I talk to Ling, my hands sweat.***

The more she thought about Ling, the more she found herself adding to the list of things she <u>believed</u> about him:

- ***Ling thinks I'm silly.***

- *Ling takes me less seriously because of my gender.*
- *Ling is threatened by me.*

The mind will do this when you sit still to work on yourself—it will try to hog all the attention. But Matilda steadied her resolve and deliberately pulled herself back to listening to her body again.

- *My heart is racing.*
- *My blood feels like it is boiling and burning.*
- *I want to tear something apart.*

Taking a few more deep breaths, she was able to remain calm and to look over what she'd written. Letting go of the belief about Ling stifling her that she had held onto for so long had hit a nerve. That said, she wasn't really okay with her lack of objectivity. Sure, she *believed* that Ling was stonewalling her rise to senior partner, but she didn't have any substantive Facts to support that belief. Was she tearing herself up over phantoms? She resolved to collect the relevant Facts and sort this business out properly, with the added goal of reducing some her stress and frustration.

Physiology Case Study Wrap Up: Both Deck and Matilda experienced intense sensations as they explored their bodies. Not all situations bring up this level of physical intensity, so you need to practice becoming more aware of the subtler sensations bombarding your body. They usually provide valuable feedback in terms of emotions, deeper wants, beliefs etc.

Practicing Physiology

Take a moment now to notice your physiology.

1. Where do you feel tense, relaxed, tired, sore, achy, or pleasant? Where do you feel high or low energy, or any other bodily sensation that you can discern?
2. Make a habit of checking in with your body several times a day. Most people find that as they become more aware of their bodies, they breathe more deeply, have reduced stress, relax and enjoy life more.

The daily practice of assessing your physiology when you're *not* stressed helps establish a baseline—so do this too. Whatever helps you to more quickly know that you need to give yourself a break from work, a particular person, or a situation is beneficial.

This concludes the examination of the Stories Direction, and the beliefs, emotions, and physiology sub directions. To put it all together, consider the practice listed below.

Practicing the Stories Direction

As I mentioned in the introduction to this chapter, Stories form the foundation of our inner universe. They are foundational in the Reality Maps we use to navigate the world, both external and internal. By decoding our Stories, we are in essence getting to know our biases and tendencies, both positive and negative. With this self-knowledge, we have the ability to become even better map builders and navigators.

I hope that by using the three sub directions, you've started to bring your own Stories into sharper contrast. I know that working with Stories continues to deepen my own understanding of myself and others, so let's take a moment to apply everything we've covered in this chapter and put the Stories Direction into practice.

1. Choose one of your beliefs and ask yourself, "Why do I believe this? How have I selectively chosen Facts to reaffirm this belief?" Consider the origin of this belief in the context of your personal history.
2. Writing practice. Take a situation you currently face and write down a sentence or two in response to each of the following questions:
   a. Beliefs: Which of my beliefs are connected to this situation?
   b. Emotions (and Feelings): What emotions do I feel when I think about this situation? How might those emotions be influencing my beliefs?
   c. Physiology: When I think of the situation, how does it make my body feel? What is my body telling me?
   d. Beliefs revisited: Considering the Facts, emotions, and physiology that I've uncovered about this situation, what other beliefs might I have?
   e. How can I evolve or develop my Stories into ones that are far more effective in my specific situations, and life?

Summary of the Facts versus Stories Polarity

FACTS ◄─────────── STORIES

Unlike the Intentions to Actions Polarity, which moves from one direction to the other, the Facts vs Stories Polarity divides the information we ascertain from a given situation into two significantly different categories. Think of the Clarity Compass Rose as a decoder ring that can help you to distinguish between fact and fiction—between the objective world and the subjective interpretations we draw about it.

Inevitably, there will be times when we confuse our judgments, beliefs, and points of view for Facts. When we act on those false Facts, the world usually fails to conform to them, and we throw our hands up in dismay. In the end, we are all human. We err even when we believe we are setting out with an open mind. But if we want to be more effective, we must be able to tell the difference between information that describes reality as it is, and information we've made up. Then we must reframe or upgrade the beliefs we've relied on and referenced all these years in our Reality Maps.

Another way to help see the relationship between Facts and Stories is to recognize that, ***the greater the number of Facts that are closely related to a Story, the*** *greater the likelihood that the Story is true*. At the same time, *a Story is never a Fact*. Any given Story simply has a greater or lesser likelihood of being on point, relevant, and helpful.

Remember when I asked you to think of yourself as being a character within the story of your own life? I'd like you to now expand that metaphor. Think of Facts as providing the setting for the character, (you). The setting can either be thought of as your life as a whole or as a particular situation you're dealing with. What setting have you, as a character, placed yourself in? You can't change the setting—the Facts—of your current life or given situation, but you can change how you interpret and respond to those Facts. You can change the Story for the better. Yes, you, playing a heroic character, can improve your ability to navigate your life and your seemingly intractable situations by rewriting your Story. Furthermore, you can change the future setting within which your character will live. Close your eyes right now: What possibilities can you imagine are available to your character?

CHAPTER 5

Creative Conversations:
A Deeper Look

I consider conversations to be the cornerstones of our relationships and necessary for being productive in the world. When we communicate, we interact with others, gain valuable feedback about ourselves, and construct our realities. Of course, when I say "conversations," I don't mean small talk. I mean the kinds of conversations that are responsible for everything we have, or don't have. From our relationships to career opportunities, from our sense of wellbeing to our capacity to change the world, in a single, humble conversation, almost anything can be realized.

Again, Creative Conversations, are those that I defined in a previous chapter as constructive communications where the Clarity Compass and imagination are directly applied with the intention of generating new and better outcomes.

If you're like most people, you have probably had "that one conversation" with the same person repeatedly. You know the one: It's that talk where you feel like you've been saying the same thing over and over again, coming at the core of the issue from every angle possible, and trying to create change, but the other person continues to engage in the same behavior. I hear about this phenomenon from people most frequently regarding their children. It's the old "How many times do I have to tell you?" tone we heard from our parents long ago, and now find ourselves saying.

The prevalence of these frustrated efforts, pushing for change or growth with no success, actually points to possibility: If you start to integrate the Clarity Compass into your daily routine and reimagine those frustrating (or dull) conversations as Creative Conversations, you will be taking a step down a new path!

Of course, Creative Conversations aren't just focused on moving repetitive conversations forward. We also use Creative Conversations with those we've never spoken to. But in any of these cases, it's helpful to think of a Creative Conversation as one you've never had before. Think: *I am now going to do something different than what I've done in the past and I am now going to expect a new outcome.*

I remember one client trying this and then exclaiming with great surprise, "Wow, I engaged in a different conversation, and I got a different result!" This happy client was in fact brilliant and very successful, and yet he was surprised by how lost he had been in his own automatic and uncreative behaviors regarding a particular conversation he had almost given up on. He was stuck thinking that "at some point these other people must be impacted by the good behaviors with which I am continuing to engage them." Thankfully, the Creative Conversation aspect of the Clarity Compass came to him precisely when he needed it, and after trying it once in his most challenging situation, he decided to put his imagination to use even more often. Creative Conversations can turn negative situations to positive, and can push already positive situations to even greater heights.

Creative Conversations are the ultimate goal of the Clarity Compass, because this level of communication leads us to a better understanding of ourselves, any given situation, and other people. By engaging at this level, we can create more positive outcomes. Creative Conversations are designed to move both you and your conversation partner further away from stagnant, Ego-anchored stances and into creative, positive, results-driven Action.

We touched on Creative Conversations briefly in the Actions Direction, and now I invite you to take on a deeper exploration in the chapter ahead. Let's walk through the process of planning a Creative Conversation, looking at what you can expect and what should you avoid.

Planning a Creative Conversation

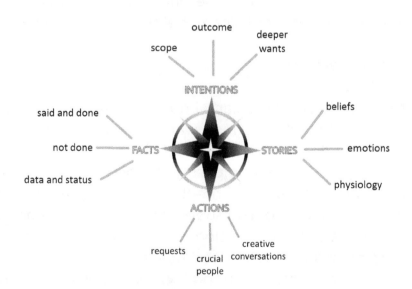

Any journey requires a map and some kind of compass or orienteering device. When embarking on the journey of a Creative Conversation, the Clarity Compass is your best tool. Remember, your goal is to use Creative Conversations to move you and your conversation partner forward. In order to do that, we'll need to bring together all of the aspects of the Clarity Compass we've discussed thus far.

Prior to having a Creative Conversation, you'll need to plan by thinking about the following:

- Your list of crucial people.
- The requests you want to make of each of them.
- What conversations could you have with key people?
- Who do you *want* to talk to first?
- Who would be *best* to talk to first?

Take your time with these questions, and make sure you've answered them clearly before moving forward.

Learning Partners

If the situation is particularly important and you are finding yourself stuck, you may want to prepare for a Creative Conversation by asking a friend or colleague for input on your Clarity Compass. I call this person a "learning partner," because the intention is not to gossip, complain, or vent, but to gain support in developing a better perspective on your situation.

For most us, it takes courage to share our Clarity Compass thoughts or writings. We are letting someone into our world. One of the reasons that it's so difficult to evolve our Reality Maps is that our critiques arise from those very same Maps. The Clarity Compass is designed to get us out of that cycle, and having a trusted friend or colleague give us feedback based on the structure of the Clarity Compass can give us the objectivity we need to more effectively question our Reality Maps. This is one of the best preparations you can do for any Creative Conversation.

Having Creative Conversations

While the preparation for a Creative Conversation using the Two Polarities is an important part of the process, it is now time to engage! What are the rules of engagement? As we move through this section, we will explore the following key tools and perspectives to support you in having the best Creative Conversations possible:

- Constructive Orientation: Respect, Curiosity, Collaboration
- Here & Now
- Mutually Beneficial Outcomes
- Imagining New Possibilities

Constructive Orientation: Respect, Curiosity, Collaboration

One of the keys to engaging in a Creative Conversation is starting out with what I call a "constructive orientation," which simply means that you will commit to working diligently to hold the most positive and productive conversation possible. Using the Intentions Direction, you'll enter the conversation by saying to yourself:

"I want to have a Creative Conversation, one where we are respectful, curious, collaborative, and open to new possibilities."

In being respectful, you honor the other person and assume that they will bring value to the conversation. You also allow yourself to be curious about the value and perspectives they offer. Finally, recognize that the conversation is being held in a spirit of collaboration, where you cultivate the experience of building a relationship and partnering with the other, even as you're moving the particular situation forward.

The Here & Now

One of the most powerful tools under the Creative Conversations sub direction is what I call the "here & now." The here & now consists of being aware of the most important dynamics of a conversation in the moment and then adjusting the conversation to accommodate those dynamics. Tracking which of the many aspects of a conversation are most critical is a skill worth practicing.

Being aware of what is going on in a conversation while having it can be challenging at first. However, when we learn to use here & now well, it increases the probability that that conversation will be more productive. To that end, we will break the concept up into two parts. First, we'll talk about developing here & now awareness outside of conversations. Then we'll talk about bringing that awareness into our Creative Conversations.

Here & Now Awareness

Here & now awareness means we are fully present in

the moment and are focusing on what is occurring as it emerges within our interactions. We are observing each of the Two Polarities as they play out within the inter-action we are having, and we are noticing and monitor-ing what's happening regarding the greater context of the conversation. In other words, we are looking at the *quality* of the communication as much as the content and focusing the way the interaction is impacting the relationship with the other person. Without here & now awareness, we are automatons, and there is no oppor-tunity for improvement or making better choices in the moment.

Practicing Here & Now Awareness

As you are reading this book, I invite you to pause to see what you notice. If you'd like, go ahead and write things down. You might notice the external environment such as what is on the wall, what noises you hear, or what people around you are wearing or saying. You might no-tice your own internal experience, thoughts, emotions, and even physiology. Or you might notice some combi-nation of the external and internal.

Pay attention to the level of detail in what you notice. You might be focused on the fine details of your external world such as a particular crack in the wall. You might notice more global themes like the setting of the room or the type of room you're in. Now do the same for your internal experience. Observe your mood and the broad-er themes in your awareness. Also pay attention to your specific thoughts, judgements, and random ruminations. In this practice, we are noticing what we notice. Stop-ping to observe what is happening can help you develop the skill of here & now awareness. Next, we will practice bringing what we notice into the conversation itself by speaking up about what we notice, and how it might be impacting the quality of the conversation.

Here & Now Conversations

Over the years, I noticed that my clients kept engaging in conversations that led nowhere. In meeting after meeting, problems were not being solved even when the stated goal of the conversation was to directly address challenging issues or problematic situations. New solutions weren't being explored, expressed, or presented.

Listening closely to the stilted, habitual, or ineffectual conversations my clients were having, it became clear that often times they weren't paying attention to the dynamics of conversations they were supposed to be engaging in at all. They thought they were; they reported to me that they were. But for the most part, they were so focused on achieving their own desired outcomes that their attention was distracted from the present-moment unfolding of the conversation. This is precisely why we need to bring here & now awareness into our conversations.

To have a here & now conversation, you need to *first* have here & now awareness of the dynamics of the conversation. As we practiced in the section above, we do this by stepping outside of what's happening and examining how we are thinking and interacting in the moment. When you do this, you'll become aware of the greater context of the conversation, the quality of the communication, the way the engagement is impacting the relationship with the other person, as well as the overall productivity of the interaction. Having here & now awareness of the conversation can be challenging since you are also continuing along in the conversation itself. Your attention is split between being engaged in the topic of the conversation and simultaneously trying to notice the dynamics of the situation.

Having the here & now awareness will give you the opportunity to make a decision as to whether you want to point out the dynamics of the conversation with the person you're speaking with. Is it helpful to bring what you're noticing here & now into the interaction that you're having? If so, which aspect of what you're noticing is most helpful? The idea of the here & now can be difficult to understand, more difficult to remember to bring into a conversation, and even more challenging to apply skillfully. However, when used well, this is one of the most powerful tools a person can use.

Of course, it's more difficult to notice what you notice during a conversation, so I invite you to practice during more mundane conversations such as interactions with a store clerk or a friendly conversation with an acquaintance. Don't save your practicing here & now awareness for your tough conversations.

<u>Here & Now versus There & Then Conversations</u>

Conversations exist along a continuum of present-ness. At one end of the spectrum are conversations dealing with one person's immediate experience with his or her conversation partner. At the other end of the spectrum are conversations dealing with things that are removed from the immediate situation, such as plans for a summer holiday or the wedding you attended last Saturday. I call the latter, "There and Then" conversations.

The following examples represent three points along this continuum:

- **Here & now**: I'm feeling a bit tired. Are you willing to talk to me about this? How is this conversation going for you?
- **There & then**: We need to have this done by September 16. The profits for last quarter were down by fifteen percent. Why should we hire Harry (who is not in the room)?
- **Between here & now and there & then**: What is the goal of this meeting? These are the outcomes this team needs to focus on. What's the best way to use our time to meet our goals? Some conversations cluster in the middle of the continuum, such as when a present desire or plan entails a yet unrealized future outcome. Another example of a conversation that falls between here & now and there & then is when we are asking if how we are using our time right now is most efficient in terms of meeting some particular future result.

While the bulk of our conversations are there & then in nature, here & now conversations often allow for greater breakthroughs. Here & now conversations can describe an interaction we're having right now. For example, I often will say in the middle of a client session, "How is this conversation going for you?" This allows us to shift, if necessary, the interaction to the topics that are most helpful. Or, we could discuss how one of us is presently feeling, or how both of us are presently relating to one another. The most critical thing is that when we are having a here & now conversation, everything outside of the conversation should take a backseat.

Here & Now Conversation Practice

The next time you get into a conversation with someone, ask yourself:

- Is this conversation moving me forward?
- Is it moving us forward?
- Is it generating new possibilities and positive outcomes?

If the answer to any of these questions is "no," try to initiate a here & now conversation by sharing your honest and tactful opinion on how the conversation is going. You could start with something like, "I'm worried this conversation isn't moving us forward," or, "How are you doing right now?" or even, "I'm not sure we're hearing each other. Can we slow things down?"

The goal is to interrupt the trajectory of the conversation and redirect it toward a more effective, generative interaction. Here & now conversations are leveraged Actions in that they often can take minimal energy in relation to the maximum positive impact they might generate. Sometimes it does take great effort to achieve the outcomes we seek, but even here we are still looking for the leveraged Action rather than the Action that is circuitous or overly arduous.

As an example, let's explore a budget conversation with a hypothetical business partner, Brandon. I share my intention: "I'd like to look at the budget together so you and I can find cuts that both of us agree are good savings." He agrees, so we meet for lunch to talk it over.

At lunch, I start off the conversation by sharing my concerns about the budget, and the places I see an opportunity to make cuts. He responds to everything I say with, "Sure, okay, that sounds good," yet I notice his eyes wandering, and he's checked his phone several times. Those are the Facts. I wonder if he's even heard anything I just said. That's my Story.

Before I begin making up too many other Stories, this is a perfect opportunity for a here & now conversation. Rather than plodding along just to get through the meeting, I pause for a moment and say: "Brandon, I notice you've said yes to most everything I've said, but I'm wondering if you've fully bought into everything we talked about?" Or alternatively, you could say, "I've seen you scanning the room and checking the time, so it's hard for me to tell how this conversation is going for you. How are you doing?"

By breaking the rhythm of the conversation, I've created an opportunity for Brandon to provide his honest experience of the moment. Who knows what I'll discover? I might learn that he's feeling stressed about a deadline that has nothing to do with me or the budget; or that he's expecting an important call shortly; or that he urgently needs to use the restroom; or even that he doesn't think I'm open to hearing what he has to say. He may not even be aware of his behavior and may feel like nothing is off. Whatever he shares, I'll learn what I can do to shift gears into a more useful conversation.

If you don't try to have the here & now conversation, especially when a conversation is faltering, it's likely you will never know what's going on with the person you are trying to make progress with, and the odds you'll get the results you are seeking will decrease.

Here & now conversations are useful when you sense the conversation is getting off-track, but you can also use here & now conversations to take a moment to express appreciation for a rewarding conversation. People love to hear: "I'm really enjoying this lunch," or, "I really value the insight you're providing." If you're inclined, you can also make the conversations more personal: "I'm so grateful for how supportive you're being," or, "I'm touched by the vulnerability you just showed."

The point is: Here & now conversations invite greater possibility into *any* conversation. Check in by asking: "Is there anything we're missing?" Encourage all participants to then use their imaginations to dream up and share a variety of potential approaches to the current interaction.

Here & now conversations work wonders because they draw attention to the quality of the conversation itself. This kind of attention is sorely lacking these days in both professional and personal environments where everyone is always multitasking, busy, and rushed. Sure, it's okay that most conversations are there & then in nature, but when you see an opportunity for a Creative Conversation, try shifting the focus of the conversation to the interaction itself and watch as new and important avenues open up. Simply naming your present-moment experience can elevate any connection to the next level.

Mutually Beneficial Outcomes (MBO)

One of the primary goals of a Creative Conversation is to make sure that all members of the discussion benefit from the interaction or receive Mutually Beneficial

Outcomes (MBO). Your orientation in the conversation should never be to overpower, intimidate, beat the other person down, or manipulate them into giving you what you want. The ideal intention of the Creative Conversation is to join with another (or others) to find positive outcomes that are satisfying to all parties.

While the here & now awareness is focused on monitoring the conversation itself, Mutually Beneficial Outcomes are specifically focused on making sure that the conversation produces the most positive outcomes for all parties involved. There may not be a solution where everyone walks away happy. Ideally, we can enter the Creative Conversation with a constructive orientation where the intention is to maximize the overall good. Accepting that not everyone is going to be completely happy every time you engage in a Creative Conversation doesn't mean you don't do your best to create MBOs. You might assume that aiming for mutual satisfaction is a first step in most situations, but I have observed hundreds of teams and partners moving forward without first taking into consideration all stakeholders or key players. I've seen R&D leaders of tech firms bulldoze decisions on feature sets for products that the marketing department didn't think they could sell. I've seen marketing leaders drive for feature sets that R&D didn't have resources to deliver. Over and over again, I see leaders in all fields set deadlines that project managers never really buy into, and never intend to deliver on.

I have seen situations similar to these improved by using the Clarity Compass to create MBOs, because calling attention to and attempting to create MBOs ensures greater buy-in, motivation, and accountability. Mutually Beneficial Outcomes are created during team meetings through the following process: each stakeholder states their desired outcomes and why they are important, each position is briefly acknowledged or restated, the outcomes are weighted in terms of their impact, and then imagination and creativity are used to try to create an outcome that best serves the team as a whole.

As you enter into conversations and relationships—professional and personal—defining a list of Mutually Beneficial Outcomes becomes critical. While your scope, problem statements, and deeper wants may be different from others, ultimately you should seek to define and agree on at least a few outcomes that will benefit both (or all) parties.

Imagining New Possibilities

Conversations can be framed in many ways: conflict-based, crucial, fierce, critical, and even collaborative. Note that most of these adjectives have a slightly negative connotation, indicating either a sense of conflict or desperation on the part of those involved. But I've chosen to place the adjective "creative" in front of all conversations because I want to create a more optimistic framework from the very beginning. Creative Conversations are ultimately about imagination and collaboratively opening up new possibilities for all involved.

Through our framing, we set the stage for what unfolds. Becoming aware of our Intentions and clearly articulating them is essential to creative collaboration. Let's look at the example of our hypothetical business partner Brandon. While I could merely say, "I want to look at the budget," it might be better to whittle that statement down further and say, "I want to look at the budget to find ways to make further cuts." Or, even more specifically, "I want to look at the budget so that you and I can find cuts that will improve our performance."

Note how infusing my Intentions into the communication immediately opens up new possibilities. Using words like "improve" sets a positive tone and sets up all parties to receive beneficial outcomes. At the same time, using the word "cuts" may limit the conversation. It may be best to say, "Would you be willing to meet for lunch next Tuesday on the budget? I want to look at ways we can improve our performance." This keeps the conversation open for items Brandon may want to bring to the budget table.

In some cases, of course, there may be no perfect way to phrase a statement or request, but our Intention is always to remain as open as we can to inviting positive outcomes.

As you initiate conversations, be mindful of how you frame them. If you notice yourself using words like "difficult" or "conflict," see if you can reframe things in a way that invites possibility and openness instead. Utilize words like "creative," "collaborative," "imaginative," or "opportunity."

You may notice that I am inviting you to engage in conversations that are the opposite of adversarial or aggressive—though I acknowledge they sometimes take place. And sure, we all have worked with someone who seems to live to argue. We are, in fact, surrounded by television shows that love to vote people off the island or out of the team. Explicit in how we invite people toward having more Creative Conversations is a here & now awareness that fosters deep listening, respect, curiosity, collaboration, as well as a spirit of safety, goodwill, and optimism.

As you focus on this orientation, your conversations are more likely to lead you toward results that were previously unimaginable.

Creative Conversations with Deck and Matilda

Our case studies, Deck and Matilda, will not illustrate all of the steps outlined above, but the following section will give you a flavor of the kinds of Creative Conversations they were able to have. Keep in mind that we are all always working along a continuum as we transform toward more clarity and effectiveness.

DECK

Recall Joe from Deck's list of crucial people. He is a much respected and admired leader who has never had trouble retaining employees. Deck reached out to him with the Intention of having a Creative Conversation that would help him to improve his situation with his employees.

Deck and Joe are now downtown, fourteen stories up, at a restaurant with a clear view of the river and an excellent selection of local salmon. They place their orders and after the server vanishes into the kitchen, Joe looks at Deck and asks "What's on your mind?"

Deck has prepared for this conversation, and though he has no idea exactly how it will end, he knows how he wants it to begin. "You're a good boss. Your people stick around. Will you let me know how it is you keep them?"

After Deck makes his request, Joe sits back in his chair and says "While I don't like to brag, I haven't lost anyone on my immediate team in a number of years."

"Years?" Deck asks. "I hope you'll share how you

manage that, because what I'm doing isn't working."

While only months prior to this meeting Deck would never have thought of risking such vulnerability, by naming his problem aloud to someone who already knows how to solve it, he's taken a definite step in the right direction.

Joe is a little stunned by Deck's honesty, but he answers, "It's not rocket science. You arrange things so that staying is in your people's best interest."

"Isn't money enough?"

"Rarely. You know, it's like any deal: you have got to work out what they actually want even if they don't know what they want. If they don't know what they want then they're gone before they figure it out."

Deck had never considered the idea that his employees might truly want something more than money, or that they deserved much beyond the money they were already receiving. If it were anyone other than Joe, he would have dismissed the idea that it was his job to figure out and provide employees with what they wanted. Deck felt a little crazy—a feeling that is common when working through our most deeply held or subconscious beliefs. But as his beliefs began to shift, he reported feeling oddly buoyant, like he'd broken through the surface of a great mystery.

MATILDA

Felicia is one of Matilda's crucial people, a fellow employee who is intimately familiar with the dynamics between Ling and Matilda. One evening after work, as the two of them were walking through the parking garage, Matilda confesses, "I don't think he respects my opinion or abilities at all. I think he thinks I'm silly."

Felicia nods unenthusiastically, clearly tired. Matilda watches as she rattles her key-fob impatiently between her fingers. *Am I making this all about me?* She thinks. *Maybe this is a prime opportunity for a here & now conversation?*

"Are you okay?" she asks Felicia.

"I'm listening," Felicia says. "I'm just neck deep in the Barrowman project."

"Is there anything I can do?"

"We do need more people on the project, so in the unlikely event that you can swing an assignment over to us, that would be amazing."

Matilda leans against her car, contemplating the possibilities. "I'd have to petition Ling for the temporary transfer."

"Well, it was a nice idea."

"No, wait," Matilda begins to smile. "I think this could help my case with him, actually. The Barrowman project is the biggest one we have; and Ling would have to acknowledge that by requesting this work, I'm both serious and capable."

"Which I think you are," Felicia says.

Matilda grins and says, "Thank you."

By being open to Felicia's fatigue, she has uncovered a path of Action that will help them both. She'd entered into the conversation with no way of seeing this path, but simply by being aware of what was happening with Felicia and offering to help, she discovered an opportunity.

Here we see a prime example of utilizing a here & now conversation to up the ante. Matilda realized that having a Creative Conversation with Felicia on the fly as they were walking through the garage was probably not respecting the spirit of Creative Conversations. It'd be more ideal to hold this Creative Conversation after she gave it some forethought and could secure an environment that was more conducive to having a good, lengthy discussion.

She had many coffees with Felicia, so to set a different tone she booked a conference room for their meeting. She reviewed her Clarity Compass notes and walked herself through each of the concepts and skills for having Creative Conversations. Matilda decided that for the requests sub direction, she would ask Felicia to have a conversation with Ling suggesting that Matilda was a serious and dedicated worker who was ready to be a partner. In the conference room, the following took place:

Matilda: 'Thanks for meeting with me today to talk about my becoming a partner and my relationship with Ling."

Felicia: "I'm happy to help. I know you've been working hard for the promotion."

Matilda: "I think it would be best to share with you some of the thoughts I've had as I've been working with this Clarity Compass tool." Matilda proceeded to walk Felicia through each of the subsections of the Four Directions. "So what do you think?"

Felicia: "I think it sounds like you understand the situation very well." She shifted in her seat, and Matilda realized she had a Story in her head that Felicia was ready to end the meeting, so in respect of Felicia's time, she would need to make her request soon. She went for it!

Matilda: "Would you be willing to talk to Ling on my behalf and let him know that I am a serious and dedicated worker and that I'm ready to be a partner?"

Note that at this point in her Clarity Compass work, Matilda has only spent time doing the work for *herself*, and that she has spent no time on Felicia's understanding of the problem. This is why we also practice the Clarity Compass for Other, which we will do in the second half of the book: To become more skillful at inviting the other person's perspective into the conversation.

Fortunately, Felicia was receptive: "Sure, I'll have a conversation with him about that."

Matilda noticed again that Felicia had shifted in her seat and picked up a pen. Again, she assumed that Felicia was ready to leave.

Matilda: "Thank you! I really appreciate that!"

Practicing Here & Now, Matilda thought, *While this is more of a Creative Conversation than I've ever had with Felicia in that I made a direct request, I don't feel like we brought a lot of imagination or creativity to it. I'm not sure we explored as many possibilities as we could.*

Matilda now shifted in her seat too, becoming slightly uncomfortable. "Before you go, let me ask you: You've mentioned that you see me working hard and that I deserve the promotion. Is there anything you can think of where I might not deserve it?"

Felicia: "No, I can't think of any reason why you wouldn't deserve the promotion. But I do think that what you wrote down for the Clarity Compass shows you where Ling might have some hesitation in granting it to you."

Matilda: "In what way?"

Even as she asked, she could see Felicia slightly gripping her chair. Matilda thought about her Facts. She felt like she had enough to support a Story around Felicia not being comfortable in the conversation. She soldiered on, despite the growing sense of wandering into unfamiliar territory. Her statement provided a number of here & now points: "Felicia, I feel like we're colleagues and good friends; and since this is an important issue to me, I want to have a conversation with you, but I don't want you to be uncomfortable."

Felicia hesitated, then said: "It's precisely because we are good friends, as well as colleagues, that I don't want to do anything to create friction between us."

Matilda: "Neither do I. Are you thinking that giving me feedback will create friction between us?"

Felicia: "I don't have anything bad to say and I do think you are ready to be partner, but people do have misunderstandings, and I just don't want to risk saying anything that you might take as being critical of you."

During your Creative Conversations, count on people not being one hundred percent direct with you. In the many 360 interviews I've conducted, asking direct questions to those who work closely with my clients means there will always be a gap between what my client is hearing from the interviewee and what the interviewee says to me. Sometimes the gap is small, but there are almost always critical elements of the equation that my client was never aware even existed. Furthermore, even people that are proud of how direct they are tend to be unconsciously protective of others and seek ways to make sure nobody is feeling attacked. For example, as overbearing and overly direct as Deck usually was, I witnessed him on a few occasions being less direct and clear in his feedback.

As the conversation between Matilda and Felicia continued, it became clear that Felicia had serious concerns about being one hundred percent upfront with Matilda as well as concerns about speaking directly to Ling on Matilda's behalf. Still, their conversation was valuable from the standpoint that it shifted to the here & now in terms of their relationship and their desire to openly communicate. They came to an agreement about the risk and opportunity sharing clear feedback with one another. They saw how it could deepen their relationship as well as help them in their careers. Before their time ran out, Matilda paused, smiled, and asked hesitantly: "Now that we've decided we're going to be more open, do you have any feedback for me on what I wrote in my Clarity Compass?"

Of course, even as she asked, she realized that in some subtle way she had been avoiding asking directly for feedback.

Felicia, smiling back and equally hesitant, said: "I think the part you wrote in your Clarity Compass about being more strategic is spot on. While I do think you're partner material now, and you do have places where you are strategic, this is a place where it would be very helpful for you to focus. You're not poor at strategy, you just don't spend enough time with it."

Matilda: "Thank you! That helps me not take it as an attack when Ling says it. And it helps me take it more seriously as something I need to focus on. What about the being a serious and dedicated worker part of my Clarity Compass?"

Felicia: "I completely see you as a serious and dedicated worker, but since we're risking giving constructive feedback, I do think that you tend to be resistant to Ling in his requests of you. I believe he can sense it and that it impacts the priority you give his tasks."

Matilda: "Yes, you can see in some of what I've written

in the Clarity Compass that I'm discovering how resistant I've been to him. So you can see why he feels like I'm not serious and hard-working?" (Here, Matilda is para-phrasing, both to make sure Felicia know she's listening, and to check her own understanding of what Felicia is saying.)

Felicia: "I'm not going to be critical of Ling, but I will just say he has an overly strong emphasis on compliant dedication to his projects. His opinions of you may be due, in part, to how demanding he is. At the same time, I think it's great that you are focusing on where you may be resistant to him."

Matilda nodded and thanked Felicia again. The wom-en parted, realizing that they had run out of time. Matilda wanted to take Felicia off the hook for having the con-versation with Ling until she had proved that she could be significantly strategic. She left the meeting elated, because she felt she had the confirmation she needed, and a renewed sense of enthusiasm around areas she needed to work on, as well as those areas she didn't. She felt hopeful that as she took on more responsibility for all the elements of her Clarity Compass, she could do things differently and thus positively shift her situation with Ling. Of equal importance was the fact that Matilda felt she had had a true Creative Conversation with Feli-cia. An unanticipated positive side effect was that she could already sense a significant difference in how they related to each other—and would continue to interact.

Creative Conversation Case Study Wrap Up: Note how both Deck and Matilda prepared for their Creative Conversations and held them in a space conducive to focusing and opening up new possibilities for better outcomes. Deck was prepared to be open minded, which enabled him to learn something and shift his beliefs. Matilda used her here & now conversation skills to be sensitive to her conversation partner's current state. Later, Matilda made her request, had another here and now conversation, and created a number of new possibilities. Both Deck and Matilda had truly Creative Conversations!

CHAPTER **6**

The Speed Compass

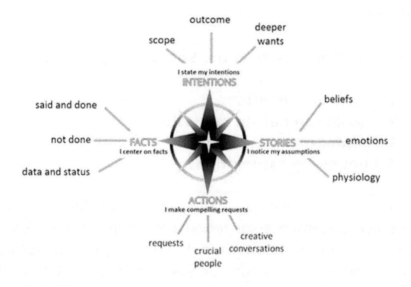

We have spent most of this book examining the Clarity Compass in depth in order for you to understand more fully each of the Four Directions. But I don't want you to think that you have to do a full analysis of every little situation in order for the Clarity Compass to be of value. There are situations that do not necessitate or allow for in-depth contemplation.

For example, you pick up the phone and a client is accusing you of turning over poor quality work or your spouse is becoming aggressive. Or, you may find yourself in the middle of a lunchroom interaction where things aren't going well. For these situations, you may not have the time to work through the polarities to the degree we have so far, but guess what: For these circumstances I've developed the "Speed Compass."

The Speed Compass is comprised of four statements that are designed to remind you of the essence of each direction, and to engage you in mental or physical activity that will move you forward in a challenging situation.

The Four Statements of the Speed Compass are:

    1. I state my Intentions.
    2. I make compelling requests.
    3. I center on Facts.
    4. I notice my assumptions.

If you're in a pinch, you can run through the above set of quick statements—or reconsider them as questions if it helps. Write your answers down on a piece of scratch paper, or even a napkin. Or you can simply keep them clearly in mind in the middle of a conversation. These statements are designed in such a way that when you use them, you will automatically recall the many sub directions of each Polarity. You'll be reminded of the various dimensions of the Compass without having to go to extraordinary lengths to make progress, or snip a minor misunderstanding in the bud.

For transformation of more complex situations and for transformation of yourself, the Clarity Compass will continue to invite you to deeper reflection; but for some situations, the Speed Compass is all you need. I invite you to go ahead and practice using these four statements in your day-to-day life.

Six Levels of Analysis

How can you know whether to use the Speed Compass or to complete an entire Clarity Compass? The best way to analyze an important or difficult circumstance is to write out a Clarity Compass specifically for that situation, using the Intentions to Actions and Facts versus Stories Polarities, as well as all of the sub directions. If the situation is particularly complex, you may feel it is worth creating secondary Clarity Compass scopes to work through. Yes, this probably sounds like a lot of work for one situation—because it is. But for conversations that are extremely important, it's worth the effort to do as many Clarity Compasses as it takes to increase the likelihood of getting positive results.

That said, it is also true that not every conversation requires a one hundred and ten percent effort. You don't have to do a full analysis of every little situation in order for the Clarity Compass to be of value. There are situations that do not necessitate or allow for full Clarity Compass contemplation. At a recent lunch, Kevin, a client who went through the Clarity Compass training nine years ago, stated, "I constantly use the Clarity Compass. I don't write it out anymore, but I consciously use the Two Polarities and many of the sub directions in a number of situations every day." I share this because as you become more practiced with the Clarity Compass, you will start to integrate it more easily and casually into your daily thinking. The model simply becomes a natural way of thinking, with more rational and emotional intelligence.

It's most effective to think about analyzing a circumstance as a range from minimal to extensive. Think about how much analysis you want to give to a particular situation. The following list provides six categories of compass applications for you to refer to. The first two categories are more about directly engaging in immediate conversations, and the latter are focused more on analysis to deeply examine Reality Maps and Blind Spots in order to imagine new possibilities:

1. **Here & Now Clarity Compass**: Entails thinking on your feet, charting the course of the conversation within the conversation itself, and thinking and speaking on the fly.
2. **Speed Compass**: Entails thinking or quickly writing out the answers to all four of the Speed Compass questions.
3. **Clarity Compass**: Entails writing out a full Clarity Compass based on the entire model—its Four Directions with accompanying sub directions.
4. **Circumnavigation**: Entails, as a separate step, stepping back and deeply reworking your entire Clarity Compass, looking for all of the nuances of how it fits together and what key factors (or people) you might still be missing.
5. **Multiple Compasses**: Use when you uncover multiple sub problems within one Clarity Compass scope.
6. **Learning Partner**: While I'm listing this as the most extensive level of preparation, many users of the Clarity Compass routinely share their thoughts around the twelve sub directions with someone they trust to provide them with helpful feedback.

The above categories represent the key decisions that you will need to make in regard to how much a particular situation warrants preparation. If time is short or the situation is not critical, a Here & Now Clarity Compass or Speed Compass will do. If you can imagine that the outcome of a particular meeting might have a significant impact moving forward, then it is undoubtedly worth spending a good chunk of time circumnavigating your Clarity Compass, or even writing out multiple Compasses. Regular practitioners of the Clarity Compass tend to be more intentional and focused in almost every moment, but when the situation calls for it they increase their preparation for the situation according to how much the opportunity warrants the investment.

From Self to Other

This completes our journey through both polarities of the Clarity Compass. My hope is that by examining your situations and your "Big Challenge", and by working through Intentions to Actions and Facts to Stories, you are beginning to evolve nimbler and more agile Reality Maps. I hope you are naming and taking Actions that lead to new possibilities and richer outcomes for yourself and others.

The Clarity Compass is reliable and it stands the test of time. As I've worked with it over the years, I've been able to develop and fine tune it—meaning that with every experience I walk a client through, I gain new perspectives. The Clarity Compass, with its Four Directions and accompanying sub directions, is adaptable to all personal and professional situations.

Most of my clients experience significant insights

and make obvious changes after going through each aspect of the Clarity Compass. They first work through the Clarity Compass for themselves and each time I am delighted.

However, there is more to it. There is a further opportunity to transform reality by running through the Clarity Compass from another person's perspective—I call this, simply, the Clarity Compass for Other, which will be the focus of the second half of this book.

Part Two:
The Clarity Compass for Other

Introduction

T he Clarity Compass for Self is designed to help you to notice perspectives you may not be fully aware of carrying. It's refreshing to shine light onto our own Reality Maps, and although illuminating our Blind Spots might feel a bit uncomfortable at first, ultimately, doing so clears the gunk out so that we can move forward on our journey more smoothly, with sharper vision, and at a wiser pace.

Now our task is to take what we've learned and apply it to understanding other people, with the goal of forming deeper and more fulfilling relationships. The Clarity Compass for Other invites you to consider the same problems, questions, or issues you've been exploring for yourself, but to approach them from the perspective of another person. And don't worry: Relearning of the Clarity Compass is not necessary! You will be taking the same route as before, but experiencing an entirely different journey.

At the beginning of this book, I posed the question: "Would you rather be right, or effective?" The Clarity Compass, in essence, is all about loosening the tight grip we tend to hold on our own worldviews. It's hard to drop your assumptions, beliefs, and biases in order to expand your perspective. But as we've seen so far with Deck and

Matilda, doing so is liberating and has the potential to set your life on a completely new and exciting trajectory. The Clarity Compass for Other furthers the work you have already begun doing on your Self by helping you learn to let go of your long-held, preconceived ideas and step into another person's shoes.

I use the phrase "Other" not to create greater separation between people, but to illustrate the genuine challenge of trying to understand a perception of the world that may be profoundly different from our own. At times, the perspective of Others does seem otherworldly. We all remember the wildly popular book *Women are From Venus, Men are From Mars*, and we know that even our closest friends and family members sound like they're speaking in code at times. While it's true that your understanding of Others will ultimately always originate from your own perspective, the Clarity Compass for Other will push you to play with fresh and unexplored vantage points. Finally, I hope that you will receive my intention and invitation to use the term "Other" as a way of honoring the life, humanity, and experience of the people with whom you are dealing.

Understanding another person—how they navigate a situation, what motivates them, and what makes them unique—will inevitably make your dealings with them more effective. It's important to apply our understanding of each person's unique tendencies, likes, and dislikes when we attempt to engage with them, especially in difficult situations. You already have an instinctive understanding of this: You wouldn't expect your mother to be pleased by the exact same holiday present you gave your nephew. You recognize that mindful interactions, like gift-giving, require a fundamental awareness that people have tastes, preferences, and motivations that differ from your own.

Let me use the example of one of my clients, Larry. Larry was working through his own Clarity Compass, hoping to improve his relationship with his boss, Rick. The problem was that while Larry was a top-notch performer, in Rick's eyes, when given any kind of constructive feedback about his work, Larry would spend a significant amount of time and effort—at meetings and in emails and voice messages—explaining the reasons for even minor imperfections. Now, I happen to also work with Rick, and I know he has zero interest in listening to lengthy explanations and justifications about anybody's imperfect performance.

As we worked through his Clarity Compass, Larry determined that his deeper want was to be truly understood. Most of us want this, but the desire in Larry was *very strong* and, in fact, was part of what made him such an authentic, humble, trustworthy, and easy to get to know person. The problem was that his transparency was getting him into trouble with his boss.

From Larry's point of view, by responding to the small amount of negative feedback he was receiving about his work performance, he was just sharing his experience. From Rick's point of view, however, these explanations were a waste of time and, contrary to what Larry intended them to be, served as evidence that he was not taking responsibility for his mistakes.

Once Larry began to work through the Clarity Compass for Other, he was able to see his own deep need to be understood in relation to the distaste his boss had for the type of overly transparent behavior he was exhibiting—and he decided to honor that difference. Larry had chosen to take the time to "step into the shoes of the other," and was therefore able to see his own Blind Spots, gain empathy for Rick, and change his approach to engaging with him in a way that mutually improved and evolved the relationship.

Empathetic Guessing: Stepping into the Shoes of the Other

The point of stepping into another person's shoes is not to lose yourself in someone else's perspective, but to engage in what I call "empathetic guessing." We use empathetic guessing when we apply everything we've learned in the Clarity Compass, especially our imagination, to try to experience another person's perspective— or to essentially guess what it's like to *be* them. When we treat people with compassion and empathy, we can remain authentic to ourselves while tailoring our Actions towards people in a way that accomplishes our mutually beneficial objectives.

Imagining *being* someone else requires effort and challenges the Ego and its point of view. It requires broadening our Reality Maps and taking into consideration other people's perspectives in ways that the Ego may initially find difficult to justify. This is because, at its worst, **the Ego experiences acknowledging someone else's point of view as agreeing with them as if they were right.** I cannot emphasize enough the powerful and unconscious influence the Ego has in defending and maintaining the Reality Maps that keep us stuck and unable to work more meaningfully and effectively with other people. The Ego always needs a check-in and check-up!

To fully step into the other person's shoes may require thoughtfulness and even research. Take any colleague or peer, for example, and spend some time defining their roles at work and at home. Consider their socioeconomic status (age, race, sex, class, etc.), their surroundings (anything from the way they decorate their home office to their city of origin), and any other details that help you get a flavor of who this person is. As you begin to get to know them, you begin to learn which details are important in the relationship you share, and which aren't.

I don't want to suggest that your estimations of others will always be spot on. At best they will be close approximations, and at times they might be ninety-five percent wrong. But even when they are off, empathetic guessing still helps by:

1. Reminding us there is another human being on the other side of the situation.
2. Alerting us to a perspective that we don't yet fully know or understand.
3. Creating a sense of compassion for the other person, even if we don't know the specifics of their perspectives.
4. Motivating us to attend to gaps in our knowledge and take the initiative to ask important questions.

The primary point in empathetic guessing is not to get too caught up on the specifics of what you've imagined, but to remember that every individual's needs, Intentions, emotions, and beliefs are just as unique and just as valid as yours. You will never fully know or understand someone else's situation, but the more you make the effort to do so, the more likely it is that you will engage in

Creative Conversations, achieve Mutually Beneficial Outcomes, and move forward.

Empathetic guessing can help you build better, more compassion-driven relationships. However, as we discussed in applying the Clarity Compass to ourselves, the danger in empathetic guessing is assuming that we are right. The more empathetic guessing (or assuming) we find ourselves doing, the greater need there is to ask the other person directly what they want and what is important to them. Whenever I practice empathetic guessing with the client, I try to estimate what percentage of what I'm saying is correct. I then check my accuracy by asking the client for feedback on my feedback. Not only does this develop my skill in assessing my own thinking, but it also reminds me that I am always susceptible to being wrong. In the end, empathetic guessing is still guessing, so it's best if you back it up with a shared examination of the situation.

Making clear to your conversation partner that you are thinking deeply about them can have a huge impact on their view of the relationship. Even if your empathetic guesses are incorrect, most people appreciate you trying to understand them, especially when you approach them respectfully and give them a chance to clarify their position. When practicing empathetic guessing within a conversation, you might say, "I imagine that you are hoping..." or "I was thinking that you might be disappointed about..."

I can't say it often enough: People appreciate feeling heard. For example, during a vacation my daughter and I took with a friend's family, my friend received several pieces of negative feedback from his family and me one night at the dinner table. My buddy is highly emotionally intelligent and resilient, but we were really piling it on.

Finally, in the middle of the noise, my daughter (who was fourteen years old at the time) turned to my fifty-three year old friend and said, "I'm so impressed with how well you're taking all of this feedback. If they were saying this to me, I would be hurt and defensive. Isn't it bothering you?"

While the rest of us had lost our way in giving constructive feedback that night, my daughter demonstrated her own empathetic guessing skills. My friend teared up and shared how grateful he was for her compassion and support.

An Example Of Not Stepping Into A Colleague's Shoes: In the corporate world, I sit in on meetings and frequently watch people talk "at one another" instead of truly listening, engaging, and making progress. During one project team meeting, I tuned into the following conversation, which was taking place between a high-level program manager, Sid, and an executive, Deborah:

> **Deborah:** "I need you to create an overall strategy for the Monthly Dashboard Update ahead of time, telling us exactly what you need from us and why, so that we don't have to run around gathering information at the last minute."

> **Sid:** "I want to reduce the time that it takes for your team to prepare for the update; but to do this, I need you to be more involved in the earlier stages of the planning process, when I'm meeting with your team."

> **Deborah:** "We do need a more strategic approach and I understand you need my involvement to create

that, but I have so many other high priority projects, that I'm just not able to meet with you and my team as much as you would like. "

Sid: "Well, I'm afraid we won't be able to stream-line the process without more of your input and team guidance."

I could tell that Deborah and Sid had this conversa-tion many times, and wasn't surprised when it continued on its irresolvable path a good while longer. Stopping the meeting, I said, "While you may be listening to each other to some degree, you aren't *fully* listening to each other. You are listening only enough to incorporate what the other is saying into your own response and feed it back to them. You aren't really allowing yourselves to hear how the other person is understanding the situation and what they are needing."

As the outsider, I could see that Deborah, the execu-tive, wanted a very high-level strategic orientation to the Monthly Dashboard Update. She wanted the overall In-tention, including broad metrics, along with a crisp over-arching design for the process and a low-level process redesign. She wanted the process to make sense from a 30,000-foot strategic level. Whenever Sid spoke, she was interpreting what he said and needed as his under-standing of the 30,000-foot strategic level.

Sid, on the other hand, was highly analytical and fo-cused on the process in terms of the data. He was in-terpreting everything Deborah was saying from his own detail-oriented tactical perspective. Whenever Deborah talked about the big picture, Sid was thinking about who had what data, and how to pull it all together for the report. He cared about what information was gathered from whom and what report was sent to whom, and especially how the slide deck was made. Whenever they got together, Sid continued to ask questions that, to Deborah's ears, seemed like minutia.

Meeting after meeting, every time Deborah said: "Fix the process at *this* level," Sid interpreted the word "this" very differently. They both needed greater clarity, but couldn't even see past their own noses to realize they were having two different conversations. Neither was listening empathetically nor making the effort to step into the shoes of the other.

As soon as I pointed out that they were having different conversations, a light bulb went off that lit up the entire room. Others at the meeting admitted that they, too, had stopped listening early on in the conversation, because it was evident that Sid needed more of Deborah's time and she didn't have it to give.

After laughing at themselves, Sid and Deborah began to practice more empathetic listening and guessing. Sid came to understand that he needed to stretch his Reality Maps to include broader, strategic ways of thinking. This is a great example of the Ego inhibiting the hearing of what the other person is saying because it doesn't fit into the Reality Maps that are already in place. Once he made that shift, the Monthly Dashboard Update changed in terms of format, process, and efficiency. As soon as Deborah understood that Sid needed more tactical guidance, her Reality Map evolved too and she pushed herself to utilize some of the time she was already allotting to Sid's meetings with her team for that sole purpose.

The lesson: Whenever we assume our Reality Maps are so accurate that we stop listening to others, we miss out on opportunities to practice empathetic guessing and miss critical points in the other person's perspective.

Emotional Intelligence

Using the Clarity Compass for Self and Other provides skills that are at the heart of what is now commonly called Emotional Intelligence. Emotional intelligence is the ability to gauge another person's emotional state, to be aware of how that person's feelings are affecting your emotional wellbeing, and to use that information to manage your own emotional state within a given situation. Your emotional intelligence deals with your sensitivity to other people's feelings, as well as your own. Emotional intelligence at the most basic level can be divided into four components:

1. Self-awareness: Noticing your own important Intentions and Stories and their sub directions.
2. Self-management: Not only engaging in Actions that are leveraged, but avoiding behaviors that are undermining to yourself or others.
3. Awareness of Others: Being mindful of the Intentions, Stories, and Actions of Others.
4. Mastery with Others: Engaging in Creative Conversations.

Emotional intelligence is quite distinct from simple intelligence. I'm sure you can think of people in your life who may be brilliant and smart, but who lack a certain degree of self-reflection, emotional, and interpersonal skills. Many of the large corporations I work with, for example, often fail to recognize this important distinction.

When they are trying to tackle a challenging problem, they will often just throw a bunch of smart people at it, regardless of their emotional intelligence. But frequently, not having the right balance of emotional intelligence and just plain smarts in the room ends up reducing the group's ability to listen and makes it difficult for people to work together towards a solid, productive resolution.

When you're in the mood for it, it's great to be around happy, positive people and to ride that wave of optimism. Of course, at the same time, we must learn to keep consistent emotional boundaries. It is much less pleasant to find your brain mirroring the emotions of someone who is angry or in pain. Instead of unconsciously mirroring them, someone skilled in emotional intelligence can check their own reactivity to the situation and tell the difference between authentic emotions born of one's own personal experience, and borrowed feelings.

None of us reaches perfect mastery in our emotional intelligence, but the Clarity Compass—with its emphasis on Intentions, deeper wants, Stories, physiology, and beliefs—helps, in part, because all of these things are central to how we manage our emotions and deal with our humanity. The Clarity Compass is designed to provide a clear methodology so that if you work with it for Self and then for Other, you will be able to facilitate your own emotional experiences, as well as those of others, with more grace, respect, and emotional intelligence.

I believe that emotional intelligence is foundational for effective and healthy functioning in the world. That we, as a society, do not focus significantly more on emotional intelligence is a tremendous Blind Spot in our collective Reality Maps—a Blind Spot that constantly undermines the human race. For example, if emotional intelligence was recognized for the foundational contribution it is to basic human interaction, it would be seen as even more important than English and math in our educational systems. In fact, my hope is that someday it will be officially taught as a subject in its own right beginning at the elementary school level. Because emotional intelligence is so foundational to effectiveness and wellbeing, my hope is that you will find the Clarity Compass a powerful tool for substantially raising your own emotional intelligence to new heights!

Practicing the Clarity Compass for Other

Throughout this book, you've been asked to complete a number of writing exercises for yourself. You will now work through the Clarity Compass for Other, writing *as if you were the person you are empathizing with.* For instance, if you are Bill and you are working on a Clarity Compass for Mary Beth, you might write: "I (Mary Beth) believe that Bill is trying to get my job."

This adaptation of the Other's point of view is key to stepping into their shoes and helps minimize the projection of your own thoughts onto theirs. For example, Mary Beth is very unlikely to write: "I (Mary Beth) am incompetent and narcissistic, but Bill is brilliant," because this kind of language typically indicates that you are allowing too much of your own perspective of your Self and of the Other to slip into your writing.

One exercise that clients often like is to take the empathetic guesses for Other that they have previously written out, and circle all of the things they've actually heard the Other say. This allows them to see what they are reporting because they have heard it directly from the Other, as opposed to relying solely on what they have guessed. Later, as we will see, they can take this phase of the Clarity Compass for Other a bit further by confirming whether or not their empathetic guesses were accurate or not.

And what of our case studies, Deck and Matilda? Not to worry. We'll continue to follow them as they take on the perspectives of the Other people involved in their journeys.

As you work through the Clarity Compass for Other's Four Directions and sub directions, please continue to use the same "Big Challenge" you used for the Clarity Compass for Self. Use your "Big Challenge" in the same way you did in the first half of the book: As you read through each sub direction, take notes on how it applies to your "Big Challenge." Then, when you get to the practices, please choose a second situation. You could even use different situations for each set of practices—it's entirely up to you. You might want to start each practice checking in with yourself in this manner, and then decide. The point of these practices is to apply the Clarity Compass and its component tools to as many situations as possible to give you the deepest and broadest grasp of the material possible. Off we go!

CHAPTER **2**

Intentions to
Actions Polarity for Other

I n exploring the Intentions to Actions Polarity for Self, I hope you gained a greater appreciation for the importance of clarifying your Intentions and Actions. You might have even experienced the natural flow that starts to happen as you begin to create clearer and more powerful Intentions, which leads to clearer and more powerful Actions. Recall from our previous discussion that having a crisp clarity of purpose drives our Actions toward the singular result of meeting the predominant needs of a given situation.

Let us now apply this same understanding of the movement from Intentions to Actions to your conversation partner (or Other) and try to imagine how their Actions stem directly from their Intentions. The clearer you can be on both concepts, the more effectively you can work together.

Intentions

You already know the basics of the Intentions Direction, but working them out for another person adds a significant new layer to an already complex endeavor. Instead of answering, 'What am I trying to make happen?' you are working to understand what the Other is trying to make happen. To do this we return to the three sub directions of Intentions, starting, as before, with scope.

Scope

As we discussed in Clarity Compass for Self, scope is the space between where you are and where you want to be. In the Clarity Compass for Other, scope is the space between where I (Other) am and where I (Other) want to be.

Applying empathetic guessing to another person's scope helps you to understand how important a particular issue is to them. Many of my clients run into situations where their own project is their top priority, but the Other ranks the same project as much lower, or not at all. Stepping into the shoes of the other person helps you see these differences in priorities, and helps you work out a solution from there.

In writing out a Clarity Compass for the Other, focus only on their scope based on your interactions with them. Imagining too far beyond the situation at hand is unproductive.

Let's see how our two case studies, Deck and Matilda, worked through their scope for Other.

DECK

Deck was working hard to keep the people who were leaving his company in mind. They were, in fact, the crux of his problem and the driving force behind his urgency to do a Clarity Compass. However, he hadn't yet tried fully taking on their perspectives. Since he couldn't possibly put himself in everyone's shoes, he chose the most recent person to leave, Lyle. A dedicated, reserved young man, Lyle had joined the firm straight out of an MBA program on the GI Bill's dime, and Deck had had high hopes for him.

As he empathized with Lyle's situation, Deck remembered back to his own younger years and the feeling of being both excited and uneasy about the future. In his youth, he had always kept the same haircut and worn carefully ironed pants, shirts, and jackets. Oh, the nostalgia. He realized that while he and Lyle were different people, in his youth he, too, had wanted more out of a career and life than money. Deck wrote:

Scope (as Lyle): This job is not everything I want in a job. I need a job that fulfills some of my other wants and needs.

Lyle had to have wanted something else. If he hadn't, he wouldn't have left. Deck was beginning to see that money wasn't everything to his employees, and because he had paid everyone well and they still left, he had to be open to other possible reasons for their departures. What else could Lyle have wanted?

Note how Deck continues to go back and forth between his old and new perspectives. Here, in the Clarity Compass for Other, you can see him still trying to move away from his off-kilter paradigm about pay, and still struggling to open up to what else Lyle might want. He is at least beginning to empathetically guess that Lyle wanted more than money, but that's as far as Deck can get at this point. That said, it's a great start!

MATILDA

Ling hadn't approved of Matilda taking on the Barrowman project, telling her that although he appreciated her enthusiasm, he thought she had enough on her plate already. Matilda knew exactly how much she could fit on her plate—Matilda could juggle a dozen plates if she had to! She regarded the entire Barrowman episode as another missed opportunity, and was concerned that her resentment might cloud her ability to write a Clarity Compass from Ling's perspective.

But, she knew resentment never helped her in the water. She knew how to let things go at water's edge and do what had to be done—dive in! Working on a Clarity Compass for the Other would be helpful, and besides, she didn't want to continue to work like this—she couldn't! So, she dove in. Ling, she told herself before writing in his voice, must have actual, genuine concerns, and some were probably rooted in Facts. With that in mind, Matilda put her hands to the keyboard.

> **Scope (as Ling):** *The problem is that Matilda is not producing work worthy of promoting her to Senior Partner. I want Matilda to contribute at a level that warrants such a promotion.*

Matilda knew that if her professional reputation were based, in part, on the quality of her employees, she would want them to be ultra-competent and produce work so strong that it catapulted the whole team into the spotlight. It wasn't unreasonable of Ling to want the same.

Scope for Other Case Study Wrap Up: Note where Deck is so focused on pay that it takes a crowbar to open him up to the possibility that other elements of a job or career might be more compelling to Lyle (and to others). At this point, you may perceive Deck's progress as minimal, but this small change nevertheless provides a toehold for him to hang more empathy on later. Witness, too, how hard it was for Matilda to separate her own feelings from the task of seeing from Ling's perspective. This level of resistance is to be expected, especially in challenging situations where emotions run high, but it is worth taking the time to calm your thoughts and apply empathic guessing. By struggling to step into the perspectives of their Other, they are better able to begin to step into a problem statement as their Other would define it.

Practicing Scope for Other

Take a moment to check in with yourself—what situation and which Other needs your attention? Beyond your "Big Challenge," is there another situation you would like to improve upon?

1. Through empathetic guessing, imagine what the situation looks like from the other person's perspective and write down a brief description of what you see.
2. Double check that you have written the situation down as if you were the Other. Did your own vantage point slip in? If so, refine the perspective.
3. Write down the scope of the problem statement from their perspective.
4. Double check to see if the problem statement you have written on the other person's behalf is scoped too narrowly, or too broadly. Recognize, too, that you might need to include a short list of sub problems.

Desired Outcomes

Recall that a desired outcome is a descriptive statement of your objectives—the more specific and even quantifiable, the better. In the Clarity Compass for Other, we're interested in discovering the desired outcomes of those we're engaging with. You may already know the vision or objectives of the Other you are working with, because these are things people are frequently expected to share. But sometimes, you may want to know more detail about the outcomes they're seeking and might simply ask, "What do you want?"

It's not always easy to ask such direct questions, but there are multiple ways to enquire into a person's hopes:

- "What next step(s) would you like to see taken?"
- "In the end, where would you like finances to be?"
- "What do you hope will come out of this meeting?"
- "What objectives are you trying to meet on this project?"
- "What is most important to you in the next hour?
- "If the release goes well, what would you be expecting to see?"
- "I'm not sure I'm tracking this conversation well. What is it you think we should focus on?"

These questions are a helpful part of any Creative Conversation and allow you to uncover the other person's Intentions without sounding confrontational. You're not going for deeper wants here; you're simply asking them for a description of their vision or the outcomes that they're trying to reach. In listening carefully to their responses, sometimes you can discern the Other's deeper wants, but usually it is best not to push anyone to share information that is too personal, unless you have a good relationship and the circumstances warrant the asking.

So, start incorporating more questions into your conversations and you'll find that when you ask people to say what they're hoping for, most will appreciate your interest and want to share. If you can't ask the Other these questions directly, do your best to imagine their perspective, based on what you already know about them. Either way, you'll make progress the majority of the time.

Now let's see how Deck and Matilda went about divining their Others' desired outcomes.

DECK

Since Lyle had already left, Deck couldn't ask him directly about his desired outcomes, so he imagined them. Deck thought carefully about what he'd wanted from a job when he was Lyle's age. It wasn't a whole lot: He mostly had wanted not to have to worry about being able to pay rent and bills. A military career had very likely fit that need for Lyle, but what else might he want now?

> **Desired Outcome (as Lyle):** *I want a job that will be stable enough for me to build my life around it, and will also be interesting enough to keep me from getting bored.*

Deck had thrown that last bit in because Lyle was a millennial, and he'd recently read an article discussing millennials' high need for personal fulfillment. Deck realized that he had started his own business in a bid to keep life interesting, so why wouldn't Lyle be looking for something similar? If Deck were looking for a job, he would be after one that was stable, interesting enough to make a long-term engagement, had good financial benefits (high salary, insurance, retirement plan), and with trustworthy co-workers. Deck smiled: He was starting to make headway.

MATILDA

Matilda hadn't given the particulars of Ling's job a lot of thought, so it was challenging for her to come up with his desired outcomes. She started her empathetic guessing by imagining Ling's job responsibilities. She started to see that as her manager, his own performance was directly linked to hers, and that meant he *had* to care about her performance.

Desired Outcome (as Ling):

- *I want Matilda to get her work done well and quickly.*
- *I want Matilda to contribute strategically to the firm's future growth.*
- *I want Matilda to bring in new clients and new work.*
- *I want Matilda to validate and implement my ideas.*

Matilda hadn't expected her empathetic guesses to fully mirror Ling's reality, but she was impressed by how reasonable these desired outcomes were. Any boss would hold similar desires of an employee. This helped her to see that Ling wanted her to succeed because that would reflect well on him.

Desired Outcome for Other Case Study Wrap Up: Note the interesting realization Matilda had concerning how easy it was to make a first empathetic guess. Note how Deck integrated some recent reading into his empathetic guessing. Both ended up with reasonable outcomes.

Practicing Desired Outcomes for Other

Let's do the work Deck and Matilda just did. Hopefully, you've already reflected on how desired outcomes for Other relates to your "Big Challenge." In these exercises,

I encourage you to use a different situation. Remember, you can either ask your Other directly about their desired outcomes, or you can imagine them.

1. Consider the situation you used in determining the scope for Other.
2. What are the outcomes your Other would want for the situation?
3. Notice how many of these outcomes might be slipping into what *you* want and eliminate them. Step further into the Other's shoes and notice if the outcome changes a bit as you more deeply orient yourself to their perspective.

Deeper Wants

Every goal we set, every decision we make, every project we start or conversation we have stems from a need or a want we are trying to meet. Deeper wants have two primary qualities: they are personal; and they are deeply rooted in us. They are what move us, what drives us. They are about what matters most to us as human beings.

Sometimes a want can be as basic and shallow as wanting your food to be saltier, but as we are examining deeper wants, we typically notice that they contain multiple layers of deeply rooted wants. Sometimes too, the deepest aspect of a deeper want resides underneath the outcome. With the Clarity Compass, we explore these layers of depth to mine a greater understanding of what drives us and makes us uniquely who we are.

Recall too from our earlier discussion, the distinction between deeper wants and situational wants. For instance, we mentioned the situational want of one young man: *I want Sarah to love me*, which came from the deeper want: *I want to be loved*. It is that deeper want we will focus on again here, but this time, the process will be even more challenging, as we are trying to uncover someone else's deeper wants.

It's unlikely you'll uncover someone's deepest wants by asking: "So, what do you want *underneath* what you're saying you want?" Not only is this type of question a bit too intimate for most people, many of us aren't even aware of what our own deeper wants are (of course, we've worked toward that level of knowing, by utilizing the Clarity Compass for Self)! As you work through this section, try to focus on what the Other's deeper needs and wants *might* be. Even if your assumptions aren't accurate, this practice will allow you to empathize with others and see that their behaviors, just like yours, are motivated by things that lie far beneath the surface.

If you *can* figure out what someone's deeper wants and needs are, you can help them get those needs met. That's right. We're not trying to manipulate or take advantage of the Other. We are trying to help them! Helping the Other usually results in enhanced levels of cooperation and greater effectiveness in the overall relationship, and thus, an improved situation. That said, for the few people who do permit you to question them about their deeper wants and needs, take a moment to appreciate the gift they are giving you. They trust you with something personal. Honor the safety that most people require for that level of sharing.

Taking the time to understand a person's deeper wants often helps us to see origins of behavior that may have, until this discovery, seemed irrational to us. For example, you might find that your mother-in-law's need to control is coming from a deep desire to protect her loved ones, or to be loved and acknowledged herself. Either way, knowing where she is coming from creates a sense of empathy for her, and allows you to avoid reacting in an emotional, knee-jerk fashion.

Just as you have been deepening your understanding of how your deeper wants drive your everyday behaviors by working with the Clarity Compass for Self, you will deepen your understanding of how the deeper wants of others drive them, by working with the Clarity Compass for Other. With these new levels of awareness and empathy, you will find new harmonious ways to work with previously unseen motivations and parameters.

Now let's see how Deck and Matilda undertake the challenge of uncovering their Others' deeper wants.

DECK

As Deck attempted to determine Lyle's deeper wants, he thought back to his own youth when he found himself in a similar situation to Lyle. Deck's military career had been cut short after an altercation with a superior officer left him stuck behind a desk for what seemed like an unjust eternity. Deck still bore a grudge against that officer. Connecting with what it felt like to be young again—probing back into his experience of his falling out and subsequent disdain—Deck dove into writing.

Deeper wants (as Lyle):

- *I want respect.*
- *I want responsibility.*
- *I want to be valued.*

Writing out Lyle's deeper want forced Deck to come out of his reverie and seriously look at what he'd written. The fact that Lyle wanted respect was now so obvious to him that he couldn't imagine thinking about him any other way. A question now nagged at him: Had he actually treated Lyle with respect?

MATILDA

Matilda knew a fair amount about Ling: He had several kids, and the oldest was in high school; his wife stayed home with the younger children; his parents had immigrated to the USA in the mid-seventies and he'd had a tooth-and-claw approach to achievement in school that hadn't made him a lot of friends. Working out Ling's deeper wants seemed pretty easy.

Deeper wants (as Ling):

- *I want to provide for my family.*
- *I want to give them the life I wanted as a child.*
- *I want to be proud of my achievements.*

Through Matilda's empathetic guessing, she tapped into Ling's high value on family. However, by focusing on Ling's family, she created "situational" wants rather than deeper wants. Almost everyone does this. So I invited her to keep what she'd written as situational wants, but rewrite them as purely deeper wants. She revised:

Deeper wants (as Ling):

- *I want to be a provider (for my family).*

- ***I want to give (my family) the life I wanted as a child.***
- ***I want to be proud of my achievements.***

Designating Ling's family as parenthetical may seem nit-picky, but for accessing deeper wants, it is important not to be distracted by the situation or other people. It's important that the focus remain solely on the individual in question and the particular things they want, rather than on how those wants affect the people and circumstances around them.

Also, Matilda realized that she was more easily able to list Ling's deeper wants in relation to his family, because in her mind, his family was the one thing that made him human. She further realized then that it would be helpful (and necessary) to look at his deeper wants as they related to work. She took the time to look back on what she'd written as Ling under scope and desired outcomes to help her explore what deeper wants he might have that he is trying to meet through work.

Deeper wants (as Ling):

- ***I want to be seen as successful.***
- ***I want to be seen as competent.***
- ***I want to be seen as the man who can get the job done.***
- ***I want to feel proud of my work.***
- ***I want to feel good about the hard worker that I am.***
- ***I want to be respected.***

Matilda thought of these as good general deeper wants for Ling, but she wanted to include more about herself in them without making them situational wants. Using parentheses to help her appreciate where Ling's deeper wants connected to her, she added:

- ***I want to be seen as (an) effective (boss).***
- ***I want to be seen as a person (leader) who gets things done through others.***

After reading the deeper wants she imagined for Ling, Matilda thought, *Who wouldn't want that? My own desire to care for people and to focus on achievement show me I have more in common with Ling that I realized.*

Deeper Wants Case Study Wrap Up: Note the powerful realizations that Deck and Matilda had as a result of exploring their Others' deeper wants. Matilda found she had more in common with Ling than she realized and Deck started to question his preconceptions and treatment of Lyle. Also note the different path they used to get to the statements they wrote, which highlights again that there is no one right approach to working through the Clarity Compass practices. Practice and develop a method that works best for you!

Practicing Deeper Wants for the Other

Now it's time to take what you've learned thus far and apply it to your own life. Again, you can use any situation that needs attention.

1. As you empathetically step into the Other's perspective, imagine what they might want from the situation. Focus on their situational want, which

relates to the particular circumstances at hand and connects the deeper want to the situation.

2. Now try to determine the deeper want below their situational want. Remember, a deeper want is one that stands on its own without any reference to the situation, so keep working to pull the equation apart.

3. As you focus on the Other's deeper want, allow yourself to experience the common bond of all humanity: The Other is a human being, who, like you, is moved to meet her or his deeper wants.

Extra Credit: Allow yourself to hope for the other person that their deeper wants are met.

Trust that taking on this perspective will make a difference in the situation and ultimately change your life, as well as theirs.

Practice Questions for Intentions for Other

We have now completed exploring Intentions for Other. Hopefully you've already applied all of the sub directions to your "Big Challenge" and by now you are feeling more comfortable with your empathetic guessing skills. Before moving forward there is one more Intentions practice you can use to pull together what you've learned:

Choose a new person for the Other role:

1. What problem are they trying to solve?
2. Practice empathetic guessing: Write out, as the Other, how you would feel about this situation. Try

to think about how the things you know about the Other might affect their behavior. What outcomes do they want?

The next step involves stepping outside the written exercise and having a conversation with the other person. This will help you assess your empathetic guessing skills.

3. Ask the Other about their Intentions. Be curious and open while listening. Check their answer against your empathetic guess. How are they different? What did you get right?

Actions

We are all dumbfounded at times by the Actions and behaviors of others. I can't tell you the number of clients that tell me they are shocked when people don't do what they would do if they were in the same situation. The fact is, we all respond and act differently, based on our unique Reality Maps. If your child got caught cheating on a test, the consequences you lay out for them might be entirely different than the consequences your own sibling might lay out for his or her child—in fact, one of you might not even believe in punishment at all. The bottom line is that we're all different and so we all act differently. These differences often create problems in our relationships, both personal and professional.

Because empathetic guessing around the actions the Other might take can be challenging, let's briefly review the Actions Direction: Actions can range from making a request you might not have considered before, to having the risky conversation you've resisted for years. They are the choices, big and small, that have the power to create your most positive, fulfilling results.

Recall too from our earlier discussion that Leveraged Action Steps are those consciously chosen Actions that will have the greatest impact in moving you toward what you want. Leveraged Actions are not about using people to get what you want, they are about identifying people who might be available for mutual collaboration and support. The opportunity now is to extend your practice of creating intentional Actions to your Other.

Similar to the rest of the Clarity Compass for Other, the goal of the Actions direction is to develop a greater appreciation for the behavior of others so that we can build more fluid and meaningful relationships, and thus engage in more effective interactions. We use empathetic guessing to imagine not only why the Other might be behaving the way they are today, but also how they *might* behave in the future.

Of course, empathetic guessing will not allow you to precisely predict your Other's future behavior. However, in articulating the possible Actions available to your Other, and considering what might motivate them to go this way or that, you open yourself up to seeing how their Actions could (and often do) differ from your own. From there, you can clear away a level of frustration or confusion, and move forward to find better ways of interacting with them.

Allow yourself to complete the picture of your Other as a whole person, decidedly separate from you. They could be just as caring, hard-working, stressed out, or joyous as you are, but the way they present those feelings could differ significantly from the way you experience them. Through empathetic guessing, you may learn that the other person has options you've never considered, but now that you're familiar with their particular situation, you can try to understand their past and potential Actions.

Remember, it is easy to mistake your own wishes and assumptions for those of the Other. Sometimes we are certain we *know* what our Other is going to do, but when we take a step back to clear our heads, we realize we have listed the things we *want* them to do. As you move through this Direction, stay as true as you can to the Other's vantage point. It may be challenging, but uncertain sympathy always trumps definite indifference. Let's now tackle the Other's view for each of the three Action sub directions: requests, crucial people, and Creative Conversations. Once again a quick reminder to keep your "Big Challenge" in mind while you explore Actions for Other.

Requests

No one is an island. Because of our interdependencies as human beings, we often need to ask one another for help—it's natural. Requests (for help) are, in fact, a reflection of living as social beings. As we explored earlier in the book, the most effective requests are those that are linked directly to our Intentions. Powerful requests are clear, actionable, and compelling. Our opportunity now is to create requests from the viewpoint of our Other.

In the Intentions Direction for Other, we found ways to more naturally and casually ask the Other, "What do you want?" In this sub direction, we envision what requests the Other might have of us (or others) in order to satisfy those outcomes and deeper wants. Remember that we can't assume the Other will make the kind of requests we want them to make—or that they'll make requests we can easily answer. We are looking beyond our narrow point of view to shed light on the things the Other *actually* needs from us, and from others. We do this because an effective relationship is one in which everyone's needs are optimally met. By using empathetic guessing to determine the kinds of requests the Other might make, we can learn how to better support their needs and requests. We can do this out of our generosity, and at the same time hope that we are on our way toward building a stronger relationship that will clear the way for them to support us as well.

Let's check in on how Deck and Matilda created their requests for Other.

DECK

Deck knew that there were several ways to get what he wanted. Usually, just asking worked. He was the boss, after all: When he said jump, people asked how high. Then there were the problems he could just throw money at, and other problems that required a harsher tactic. He'd had more than a few moments where he'd had to put the fear of God into people.

Deck knew that his Other, Lyle, did not have the same kind of personality or level of power. His options were much more limited. If Lyle was unhappy about the way the job was going, he would have had to ask Deck for more responsibility and more respect. Deck proceeded to write down the requests Lyle might have had to make of him:

Requests (as Lyle):

- ***Deck, would you be willing to give me more responsibility?***
- ***Deck, would you be willing to show me more respect?***
- ***Deck, can we talk about how you could show me that you value me?***

Could Deck realistically expect Lyle to march into his office and demand to be treated better? Probably not, but by going through the process of imagining Lyle's requests, he developed more empathy for him, and gained more insight into why people, like Lyle, might not be talking to him directly.

MATILDA

Matilda was beginning to develop a small stirring of empathy for Ling, a man who shared so many of her own motivations. She had little trouble imagining what requests he could make of her to achieve his goals.

(As Ling):

- *I will ask Matilda to discuss her reports with me.*
- *I will request that she set and meet reasonable goals.*
- *I will continue to ask that she become more strategic.*

Matilda realized that if she were Ling, she might request more from her direct reports, especially if they were not meeting expectations, as Matilda hadn't been (according to Ling). In our conversations, Matilda explained that she did exceed expectations on the important objectives and client delivery, but wondered if she was intentionally not following through with Ling's busy work in hopes that he would stop giving such work to her.

As she worked through this portion of the Clarity Compass for Other, she became more willing and able to understand why Ling saw her as someone who was not following through. She also realized that his requests for her to be more strategic seldom included items that were actionable—he generally just made the broad request to *be more strategic*. She then thought, for the first time, that Ling seemed to be sending a confusing and contradictory message: Matilda should not only be thinking more along the lines of "overall strategy," but should also be following through on every detailed assignment he gave her. She realized that from Ling's perspective, the responsibility of engaging in both details and strategy, though not part of everyone on her team's job description, was part of hers.

Request for Other Case Study Wrap Up: Note how Matilda is becoming more "in tune" with her Other, and is uncovering powerful, new realizations about their working dynamic. Deck is unexpectedly realizing the probability that a dramatic power dynamic was affecting his interactions with employees, especially in terms of his receiving requests and feedback.

Practicing Requests for Other

Let's take a moment to explore the requests of Others in your own situation. Since you've already had your "Big Challenge" in mind as you worked through requests, I encourage you to use a new situation for these exercises:

1. Think of a situation you would like to improve with an Other. You might use the same one you used in the scope for Other practice.
2. Simply ask yourself: If I were them, what would I ask me to do? Some clients find this a fun exercise, as well as one that helps them to more easily get into the shoes of another person.
3. Think of another person and ask the same question.

Crucial People

As we discussed in Clarity Compass for Self, crucial people are folks we already know or people we have yet to meet who could powerfully contribute to our creating positive results. Now our task is to use our empathetic guessing skills to consider who our Other might consider crucial. Trying to determine the crucial people in the life of the Other allows us to even more fully step into their shoes. As we look around at the landscape of their lives (with a special emphasis on the situation we are seeking clarity on), we may more fully understand the perspectives they have, the pressures they are under, and the opportunities they may be trying to take advantage of or those they might be missing.

While your own list of crucial people may be quite lengthy, when stepping into the shoes of other people, it's typically not worth our time to make an extended list. It is much more helpful to imagine the kinds of people the Other might seek out and list a few names.

Now let's see how Deck and Matilda identified their Other's crucial people.

DECK

Lyle's best move, as far as Deck could tell, was to swallow his pride, keep his head down, and cautiously put out feelers for a job with another company. Yes, Deck realized, that was exactly what had happened.

As for imagining Lyle's crucial people, Deck could have created a list of all the people that Lyle might have reached out to for new employment. He could've also included people around the office that Lyle might be seeking out as confidantes. However, this would have taken too much time without bearing much result. What mattered most in terms of Deck's Clarity Compass was simply the fact that Lyle had probably created a list of people that he could reach out to for a new job. More importantly, Deck realized that most of his employees probably had a similar type of list.

This reality, of course, made Deck nervous. The old pun popped into his head, "You're not paranoid if they really are after you," and while he could laugh at himself, he did feel varying degrees of paranoia, concern, and sadness. By this time, Deck was opting for less denial and more clearing out of his Blind Spots, but significantly shifting our Reality Maps usually brings on a normal and expected grieving process. Be prepared.

MATILDA

Matilda decided that it would be most useful to explore the crucial people that Ling might reach out to, as they related to her own development. Matilda wrote (as Ling):

- ***I will ask some of the other partners to support me in developing Matilda's ability to be more strategic and bring in new work.***
- ***I will network with some of my professional associations and introduce them to Matilda.***

After running through Ling's crucial people, Matilda realized that he had not yet brought in anyone to support her. She thought of several explanations for this. First, he didn't care enough to ask others. Second, he had given up on her, so why ask others to extend their energy? Finally, he thought that he alone was responsible for all of Matilda's development.

While she couldn't be one hundred percent certain about the real reasons behind Ling's not enlisting the support of others, it seemed important to note that so far, he had been developing her without any support she was aware of. After a week of contemplating this, she came to believe that maybe Ling felt that enlisting other people's help would be a sign of weakness on his part. It was likely that he thought he should be able to manage her performance on his own. In the end, while it was likely he cared about her performance, his pride was getting in the way of asking others to help her.

Crucial People for Other Case Study Wrap Up: Note how quickly Deck realized for the first time that most of his employees were, like Lyle, probably reaching out and longing for something better. Note it took a bit more time for Matilda to process this step. You never know what the insights will be or where insight will arise while working through the Clarity Compass. The key is to allow your imagination to play with nuances of situations and others.

Practicing Crucial People for the Other

Now it's time to explore the crucial people for an Other's situation. Determine which situation and Other are presently most in need of your attention or review, and then do the following:

1. Think of *someone other than yourself* that the Other might ask for support in this situation. If you were them, who would you ask for support?

2. Refer back to the requests section to explore what your Other would ask of these crucial people.

Sometimes this is an illuminating exercise in that the person you think of might be a person that you could enlist for support, or he or she might be someone you would encourage the Other to reach out to.

Creative Conversations

Empathetic guessing is an important skill in all aspects of the Clarity Compass for Other, but it is particularly important for Creative Conversations since this is where the rubber meets the road. Remember that Creative Conversations are those in which you are actively intending to generate new possibilities and mutually beneficial outcomes. Doing so requires that you put yourself, as much as possible, in the shoes of others. Witnessing the Other in conversations makes us more likely to see where they are using Creative Conversations, and where they aren't.

As a reminder, Creative Conversations are constructive communications where the Clarity Compass and imagination are directly applied with the Intention of generating new possibilities and better outcomes. They lead us to a better understanding of ourselves, the situation, and other people. Our challenge now is to view the Creative Conversation from the viewpoint of the Other.

Primary Benefits of Creative Conversations for Other

When you extend your focus beyond Creative Conversations for Self to Creative Conversations for Other, it helps you to:

1. Think through how to best approach the Other. Not everyone likes to be approached in the same manner. Tailor your approach, and the more amenable to conversation an individual is likely to be. For example, many introverts prefer to have advance notice on topics so they have a chance to sit and think through them before conversing.
2. See more clearly how the Other might be trying to approach you, based on their own Reality Map. Many people don't take into consideration that the other person might be reaching out in some way that does not register on their radar.
3. Appreciate where they're coming from as well as giving the other person credit for the efforts they have made.

Ask yourself: "What kind of conversation might my Other be trying to have with me where I'm just not seeing their effort?" See ways that you might be shutting down opportunities for the Other to approach or be effective with you. Seeing how we make ourselves difficult to approach is difficult to assess on our own, but it's worth exploring. It could even be worth asking the Other directly how receptive to communication they perceive you to be.

As we did with the Clarity Compass for Self, we will have an initial planning session with Deck and Matilda, but we won't reveal their actual Creative Conversations until they've gone through the Facts vs. Stories Polarity. For now, Deck and Matilda are not having the conversations, but simply trying to think of how Lyle and Ling might approach them for a Creative Conversation.

DECK

Deck had already guessed that Lyle's primary issue with working for him was that he wanted respect—most of us do—but he still had to develop a plan for a Creative Conversation from Lyle's point of view. Because this was an exercise, and Lyle wasn't present, Deck started by imagining what Lyle might think about having a Creative Conversation with him.

> **Deck (as Lyle):** *Since I'm pretty sure Deck won't be excited if I go in there and ask him to be more respectful with me, I will go and talk to Deck about how hard I'm working, how well my projects are going, and how I'm handling the client responsibly. Then he'll see what a professional I am, how dedicated I am to the firm and to him and how worthy of respect I am.*

I happened to be in the room with Deck while he wrote out Lyle's words. "I can feel my stomach starting to tighten," he said, going pale. When I asked him what was up, he said, "Lyle had every one of those conversations with me. He even mentioned that he saw himself as a professional, dedicated to the firm and to the vision I was trying to create. Lyle even told me—and I didn't realize until now how serious he was—he said that he thought he was the kind of person that I would value."

Deck realized that Lyle had tried to have a Creative Conversation of sorts with him, but that he had repeatedly shut them down.

MATILDA

Matilda's view of Ling had steadily been evolving and she was beginning to see him in a different light. More writing in Ling's perspective would only improve her understanding of the situation.

Matilda (as Ling):

- *I will talk to her about how she can be more responsive and create a track record of getting her projects done.*
- *I will send Matilda my own strategic ideas and try to collaborate with her on what the best course of action could be.*

Matilda realized that many of the Actions she came up with for Ling represented behaviors that annoyed her. Being empathetic, she found she could reinterpret almost everything in a new light. Overbearing levels of busy work and micromanagement? Perhaps this indicated just a poorly constructed impulse toward trying to improve her productivity. Telling her that she wasn't thinking strategically? His choice of phrasing might have lacked finesse, but she *did* need to focus on the future and broaden her thinking. Sending her his ideas and feedback on almost everything? A second opinion is always valuable. Maybe he was trying to be inclusive and engaging with her. Honest collaboration could be good for them both.

Creative Conversation for Other Case Study Wrap Up: Clearly, working through the Clarity Compass in Lyle's shoes was confronting for Deck, but it was also enlightening. By doing this work, Deck was gaining the opportunity to make significant changes moving forward. For Matilda, this exercise once again provided her with new interpretations of Ling's behavior—almost to the point where she felt like she was describing and getting to know an entirely different human being.

Practicing Creative Conversations for Other

Now let's explore your own situations through the lens of Creative Conversations. Once you have your situation and Other in mind, keep things as simple as possible:

1. What is the main challenge?
2. Imagine being the other person.
3. With the points listed in the "Primary Benefits of Creative Conversations for Other" section in mind, ask yourself: "If I were them, what would it be like to approach me for a Creative Conversation?" Write a sentence or two for each point.

Practice Questions for Actions for Other

We have now completed the Actions for Others Direction. I hope you have experienced breakthroughs similar to those of Deck and Matilda. Again, we will be taking a deeper look into Creative Conversations once we complete the Facts vs. Stories Polarity for Other, but for now, let's wrap up Actions for Other with a final practice session.

1. Writing Practice: For your selected situation:
    a. As the Other, write out possible requests you might make.

    b. As the Other, write out a list of your allies and other crucial people.

    c. As the Other, write out ways that you think you've tried to reach out and have conversations with Others (in this case, remember, Others includes you).

2. Continue thinking about another Other and explore:

    a. What are their Intentions? In pursuing their goals, what Actions are available for your Other to take?

    b. Practice Empathetic Guessing: Write out, as the Other, how you feel about taking Action on each option. Do any of them serve the deeper wants and needs you've imagined for the Other? What makes one option more or less likely to be your Other's eventual choice?

Extra Credit: Take the next step and ask the Other about their plans. Check their answers against your empathetic guesses. Which answers differ? Which did you get right? This exercise is a great way to test your empathetic guessing and find ways to improve it.

Summary of Intentions to Actions Polarity for Other

Throughout this chapter, we've explored the Intentions to Actions Polarity for Other by learning the art of empathetic guessing so we can better step into the metaphorical shoes of Others. You looked at the way your Other acts and worked backward from those behaviors to imagine the Intentions (scope and desired outcomes) your Other is working to fulfill. You took a few great leaps of imagination to explore their deeper wants and needs, and reminded yourself that your Other is a full, autonomous person trying to succeed, just like you are. You were able to recognize in them the humanity you share, which will likely make engaging with them in the near and far future much more positive and effective.

Finding a common humanity between your Other and your Self fosters an empathy that you can use in Creative Conversations to move the situation forward, and once you have a reasonably good idea of what your Other needs, you'll be able to help them meet those needs. I guarantee you will be surprised at the difference all of this makes in your outcomes.

Once you are clear on where your Other wants to go and why, it's natural to think about what Actions they can take. As you step further into their shoes, you will better see how they might view you and why they approach you as they do. It's possible you'll think of ways to make yourself more approachable. Your new perspective might also give you a clearer sense of what Actions you can take to serve them.

Helping your Other fulfill their needs is the part of the Clarity Compass for Other I often see the most pushback on: "Why should *he* get to feel comfortable while I'm still struggling?" is a common refrain.

But the truth is that if you approach your relationships from the standpoint of "my happiness is always the most important thing," they will eventually crumble under the weight of your Ego's sense of scarcity. People are much more likely to help others if they feel like they're in a safe position. People with met needs tend to be more generous, more forgiving, and more likely to take chances on new opportunities. You want your Other to have their needs met. Operate out of a stance of abundance, and you might find not only is there plenty to go around, but also that your Other's happiness will directly affect your own.

The Intentions to Actions Polarity for Other provides a framework that invites you to understand the other person more fully and deeply. If you understand your Other in this way, you increase the likelihood of having a more mutually satisfying and effective relationship with them.

CHAPTER 3

Facts versus
Stories Polarity for Other

The primary Intention for the Facts vs. Stories Polarity for Other is to take on the perspective of other people so that we can better understand where they're coming from and improve our interactions with them. Wouldn't it be a beautiful world if we could all just walk in each other's shoes for even an hour? When we try to step into another's shoes, we are in essence exploring their Reality Maps and Blind Spots. And just like exploring your own Reality Maps, as we did in section one, one of the keys to understanding the Reality Maps of the Other is to discern the differences between "Facts" and "Stories."

What would the Other most likely determine to be the "objective facts" in a given situation? How do their Facts differ from yours? More importantly what "Facts" would they choose to emphasize, and what Stories would they construct based on the Facts they have amassed? The differences and similarities between you and your Other range from huge, world-shifting differences, like religious beliefs or political biases, to tiny, mostly insignificant details, like a preference for text over email or phone calls. It's hard to tell what will be important in your situation.

You'll have to practice discernment to determine what matters in any particular interaction, and what can be considered background noise.

Over the course of this chapter, we'll explore the Facts vs Stories Polarity as a powerful tool for taking on the perspective of Other. Some people find it easier to start with the Facts for Other and then go to the Stories for Other, and some prefer to step into the Stories for Other and then move to the Facts, mainly because it is human nature to understand life through stories. Once we have access to the belief systems that are upholding the Other's Reality Map, it becomes easier to point out the Facts or observations they might find important. Over time, you'll discover whether it's easier for you to start with Facts or Stories. In this case, we will start with Facts for the Other.

Facts

People often approach the Facts Direction for the Other by saying, "If the facts are facts because they are objective and observable, the Facts that I have will be the same Facts they have." But it's never that simple. When exploring the Facts Direction from the perspective of another, we are less interested in determining the "objective facts" and more interested in seeing which of the facts they choose to emphasize.

Most people fall into the trap of mistaking and naming their own Facts as the same Facts the Other would name. While there is probably some overlap, the primary difference between your Facts and those of the Other is not the Facts themselves, but those you choose to notice and prioritize versus those they choose to notice and prioritize. Gathering the Facts and understanding the weight of them from the Other's perspective is one of the most crucial activities of the Clarity Compass.

One of the best ways to discern the Facts that your Other considers more relevant is to listen to what your Other focuses on. Let's use an example to illuminate the point: Maria is a friend of yours who often describes herself as "rigid." It's hard to know why she thinks of herself that way, but she has told you that her parents made her practice the violin three hours a day when she was a child. So as you step into her shoes, it would be easy to assume that she would attribute her rigidity to the fact that she was required to practice so much. However, if you later hear her say that her life was highly regimented because her parents were both in the military, you may decide that the Facts related to Maria's rigidity would be more attributed her military upbringing than the violin practice. The point is that we are listening to Maria to determine the Facts that she might focus on when she examines her story about being rigid.

Remember that most of this is a story from your perspective. The only things that are Facts to you are that she told you that her parents required her to practice the violin three hours a day, as well as that they were in the military. From her perspective, it's a Fact that her parents required her to practice the violin three hours day and were in the military.

To get the most out of any Fact-exploring process, you need to develop a genuine interest in where your Other puts their energy and effort. This is about noticing the Facts that they notice, and it cannot be done in a casual way. Remember that you're working out the Reality Map of another person, with all the complexity and compassion that effort entails, and your efforts must be grounded partially in Facts. Reaching consensus on Facts, particularly in times of conflict, is key to moving toward your goals.

As you work towards an uncovering of and a consensus on the Facts, a number of shifts begin to take place:

- You find that you agree in a number of ways, i.e. you reach common ground.
- Where you disagree on Facts, it is usually possible to define that disagreement since it's usually a case of either having different memories or different vantage points.
- You discover Facts you were either unaware of or had not valued appropriately.
- Your Other discovers Facts that they were either unaware of or had not valued appropriately.
- Agreeing on the Facts often creates a spirit of co-operation.
- Sometimes, where confusion around the Facts was the source of the problem, the situation resolves itself.

Because Facts are observable, they provide easy access to points of agreement or to missing pieces of information. I once worked on a negotiation between a pair of warring functional teams. After much heated debate, one of the parties was reviewing their Facts Direction and mentioned a relevant Fact about a particular shipping contract they had signed with a Chinese company. The opposing team went silent. This was a Fact they had never encountered before, and it so happened that this Fact ended up changing the game completely. After they got over the frustration and disbelief that this Fact had never been shared, the atmosphere in the room became celebratory and the two organizations were able to reunite.

The Facts we focus on and share make a difference. Spending time reviewing and agreeing on those Facts is a worthwhile investment of time.

The most important thing about Fact gathering is that it sticks to observable behavior and evidence. The video camera approach, as you recall, is essential to understanding the Facts of your personal situation, and it is just as crucial when Fact gathering as your Other.

Now let's explore the three sub directions of Facts through the lens of the Other. One quick reminder, keep your "Big Challenge" in mind as you continue, starting, as before, with said & done.

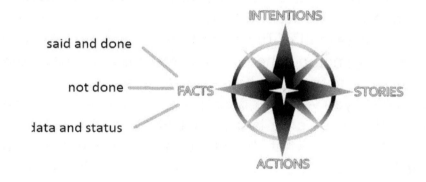

Said & Done

The purpose of this sub direction is to get clear about what was *actually* seen, heard, felt, or experienced. Remember the metaphor of the video recorder. What is actually said and done can be recorded on the video, but as we discussed earlier, each of us is holding our video camera at a different angle and perhaps recording in a different room. The challenge in this section then is to look through the lens of the Other's video recorder.

When you step into the Other's shoes, focus your attention on the issue at hand. Look for Facts he or she would likely have access to and would likely choose. For instance, there is no possible way for your Other to know you've complained about her to your brother. She was not there, and as long as your brother didn't spill the beans directly to her, chances are she won't know you think she's been acting foolish lately in regards to finances. However, if you've told her directly that you're anxious about the way her company is handling small investments, that is information she definitely has and she may now choose to select and classify this information as a critical Fact.

You don't need to restrict your said & done list to only the things you've told this woman directly—she's probably seen several of the same things you have. The key thing to remember here is that she may not have the same information you have, just as she might have information you've never been privy to. The best you can do in the latter case is use your imagination to empathetically guess what she might have access to that you don't, and later try to confirm what your Other may or may not know.

Finally, there are two more questions to keep in mind:

1. What filters and biases does your Other have?
2. How will that color their view of the said & done?

Now let's see how Deck and Matilda did capturing the said & done of their Others.

DECK

Deck was still reeling from his epiphany that Lyle had tried indirectly to reach out to him about wanting to be valued, and had probably been looking to leave for months. Hoping to gain some clarity on the situation, Deck was ready to make a list of Lyle's relevant said & done items. He took a breath and started to write down details of some of the interactions they'd had before Lyle's departure, (as Lyle):

- *I told Deck that "I didn't have enough time to finish a project."*
- *Immediately after telling him that, he told me to "get it done anyway."*
- *I stayed in the office until past midnight to finish it and email it to Deck.*
- *The next day, Deck brought me into his office and pointed out that "one of your objectives was poorly written."*

Seeing this list of Facts from Lyle's perspective, Deck's first reaction was: "The fourth point was true: one of the objectives was written poorly and if Lyle was going to grow he needed to know that. If you look at any professional sports coach, they give critical feedback. They let their well-paid professional athletes know what they've done wrong and how they can improve."

This "Be a Professional" philosophy was important to Deck. He would often say to me, "Would an infantry man ask his sergeant to be nice to him? Would a real professional athlete say to their coach, 'You give me too much negative feedback'? If they did, they would be asking to be chewed out. My people need to learn to be professionals!"

I let Deck vent for a while, he then looked again at what he had written. While I could see he wasn't ready yet to give up his 'professional' line of thinking, he kept reading the sheet over and over again. He was beginning to see that he was often too quick to criticize and too slow to praise other people's efforts. In the end this increased the likelihood of people leaving, whether he liked that Fact, or not.

MATILDA

Matilda felt she was making great strides on the Clarity Compass she was working through for Ling, so she enthusiastically took on the task of exploring his list of said & dones. As Ling, she wrote:

- *I told Matilda that she needed to think more strategically.*
- *I told Matilda that by not thinking strategically, she was damaging her standing in the firm's hierarchy.*
- *I gave Matilda several projects she has not completed.*
- *I told Matilda "I became a partner through making my projects more strategic."*
- *Every day, I would ask my boss if there's anything else that he needed from me.*
- *Every week I would meet with my boss for at least two hours for reviewing my projects.*

Staring at Ling's said & done list, Matilda thought

about all of the ways she'd felt oppressed by him: the mediocre reviews, the time-wasting meetings, the worthless projects. She'd thought he was winding her up until she gave in and left the firm, but in writing down what he might say in terms of said & done, she now saw that in his mind, he was developing her. From his point of view, he wasn't micromanaging her; rather, he was trying to get her to engage with him like he engaged with his boss.

Said & done for Other Case Study Wrap Up: Once again, Deck and Matilda had different reactions to a sub direction. Deck was not willing to own the negative impact of his behaviors just yet. He had significant work to do in terms of fighting back an old pattern of thought on professionalism. Matilda, on the other hand, easily understood how Ling might sincerely believe he was doing nothing other than trying to be helpful. Matilda was willing to see how from Ling's perspective, he was trying to be helpful and develop her even though in the end this perspective highlights, and even justifies, some of the ways that Ling has made her wrong.

Practicing Said & Done for the Other

For this practice we are not going to try to resolve any particular issue. We are just going to practice thinking about what other people might be noticing about a situation. Think of a situation where another person might be frustrated, and try to answer the following:

1. If you were the other person in that situation, what might you think were the most important items to add to a said & done list?

2. Think of another frustrated person and list the said & done facts that they would name.

Not Done

As we discussed in the first half of the book, one of the main reasons we become upset or disappointed with others is often rooted in what a person did not do (Fact) in relation to what we expected them to do (Story). When what was "not done" is causing problems, it's usually because expectations are not being met.

Accounting for the not done part of the Clarity Compass is challenging when we're working on it from our own perspective, but it is significantly harder when we're taking on the Other's perspective. Often the not done for Other is something they expected us to do, but it might not have occurred to us to take Action. For example, let's say we are showering a significant other with gifts. We might feel good about our generosity and see it as nothing but an expression of care and affection. However, if the significant other has a deeper want for being showered with praise rather than gifts, we've missed supporting them and fulfilling their deeper want. Because we see ourselves as caring and expressive, it is easy to miss the opportunity for demonstrating a particular kind of care and interest that the Other is wanting.

As you can see, overcoming our own bias for what is expected of us is a convoluted process, and should be approached carefully. Let's see how Deck and Matilda handled the very challenging completion of not done for Other.

DECK

For Deck, the not done exercise revealed one of the most likely and primary reasons for Lyle's (as well as that of many other employees) departure: Employee expectations were not being met. Once again, Deck put himself in Lyle's shoes and made a list of the ways in which Lyle, and others, might have felt shorted:

- ***Deck never thanked me for completing tasks or for finishing them by deadline.***
- ***Deck never thanked me for completing any project.***
- ***Deck didn't ask how long any project took me.***
- ***I didn't tell him how long I worked on projects.***
- ***Deck rarely asks about my responsibilities outside of work.***
- ***I didn't bring up any of my non-work plans.***
- ***Deck never acknowledged what was done well.***

Note that Deck included the word *rarely,* which qualifies that statement as a Story rather than a Fact. Regardless, he realized that he almost never asked his employees about their private lives, and so knew very little about their outside interests and passions. He began to wonder then if any of them had untapped skills and talents that, if approached in the right way, might become an asset to the company. The more he thought about the "wasted opportunity" to enrich everyone's work lives, the more he began to open to the idea that he had to do more to keep people around.

Notice that Deck's reaction centered primarily around how missing out on the personal aspects of people's lives might be a disadvantage *to him,* because he is the type of person who looks for every advantage possible. That is to say, Deck had found a way to temporarily "ignore" some of what he had been uncovering in terms of the impact of his lack of professional acknowledgement of Lyle and others.

MATILDA

Matilda was nervous about creating her own not done list. She was afraid it might be more incriminating than she wanted. As Ling, she wrote:

- ***Over the last year, Matilda has not completed twelve projects by the deadlines that I had given her.***
- ***Matilda does not ask me to review her projects on a regular basis.***
- ***Matilda did not look me in the eye and got angry when I gave her a negative review.***
- ***Matilda does not ask for ways that she can help me out.***

Similar to Deck's use of the word *rarely*, Matilda used the word *regular,* which is Story not Fact. Nevertheless, Matilda now realized, feeling shame like Deck had, that the busywork she'd been complaining about was likely Ling's attempt to provide her with shorter and easier tasks that she could perform well and proudly build her reputation on.

In the back of her mind, she had always felt this work was demeaning: Why were Ling's expectations of her so low? But since she also knew that she hadn't been meeting his expectations so far, she assumed he might have been lowering them out of necessity. This was embarrassing, but now she was pretty sure what the problem was and felt confident that she could figure out a way to fix it.

Not Done for Other Case Study Wrap Up: Both Deck and Matilda made significant progress just by exploring not done for Other. Note how Deck is starting to let go of his obsession with employee pay and "professionalism"—two factors that have been leading him astray all this time. He is instead starting to recognize and accept some of the deeper wants and interests of his people and how he didn't help them in their quests to achieve what they were seeking. Matilda came to an embarrassing realization, but it gave her something concrete to work on.

Practicing Not Done for the Other

The Intention for this practice is to more deeply understand how we might "fail" to meet others' expectations without even realizing that their expectations were so much different from our own. As we know, our Ego can be highly resistant to acknowledging what other people expect from us and why, but as we practice this aspect of the Clarity Compass for Other, our emotional intelligence will grow. We will become better at empathetic guessing, and thus more effective and engaged with others. Assuming you've already worked with your "Big Challenge", let's continue to practice using not done:

1. Think of a situation where people were expecting you to do something, but you didn't do it.

2. Whether you thought you should've done what they were expecting you to do or not, step into their shoes and try to understand why they held these expectations. What context or surrounding circumstances gave them the sense that you should take the Actions they thought you would or should?

Data & Status

Recall that data & status are the numbers, titles, and labels that we usually gloss over as Facts because we assume that we've already taken them into account. It is probably safe to assume that the Other does the same, but no matter what, it pays—and I'm not speaking financially here—not to overlook data & status.

The data & status information that matters most to your Other has usually been delivered in the form of dollar amounts or other financial statistics, or in terms of the length of time they've spent on a project. The numbers or statistics your Other emphasizes might overlap with yours, or not. Either way, taking a good look at what particular data the Other is citing or highlighting in any given situation can lead to fruitful insights and conversations.

Let's see how Deck and Matilda worked through their data & status for Other challenge.

DECK

Because Deck knew so little about Lyle's situation outside of work, he wasn't entirely sure of what kinds of numbers would matter to him. Did Lyle play sports, own dogs, binge watch the same HBO series he did? He had no clue, but he could at least empathetically guess at

Lyle's work-related data & status. He came up with the following (as Lyle):

- *I've delivered eleven projects on time, and only one project late.*
- *Deck has given me sixty-four pieces of critical feedback, and three pieces of positive feedback*
- *Deck has asked me about my personal life zero times.*
- *Deck has told me zero times to take some time off because I worked hard.*
- *My salary is 9% above industry standards.*
- *I've had five headhunters call me in the last six months.* (Here, Deck is guessing, but somewhere between three to seven calls from a headhunter in six months was reasonable to expect for Lyle's position.)
- *I have three colleagues that would hire me if they had an open position.* (This fact, too, required empathetic guessing on Deck's part, but again, this is precisely what the Clarity Compass for Other expects and encourages: The Clarity Compass for Other focuses on the kinds of Facts that are likely for the other person. This approach allows us to take those initial few steps in the other person's shoes. While we hold these assumed Facts lightly at first, when it seems we've landed on a few that "stick," we continue our walk in the Other's shoes, checking out further these lightly assumed Facts.)

Deck had trouble assimilating everything he'd written under the Facts Direction for Other—the list was long and he was not adjusting easily to stepping into some-one else's shoes. Feeling the impact of the work he was doing, he pleaded fatigue and the urgent need to get a few things done, so we took a small break.

MATILDA

Matilda was frustrated too. She had had enough Facts for one day, but decided to push through. She wrote (as Ling):

- *Matilda has been with the firm for seven years.*
- *Matilda has been under my supervision for five years.*
- *Only two of Matilda's seventeen projects have been significantly extended by winning more work.*
- *Twelve clients have asked Matilda back for $1- $3 million project. Four have asked Matilda back for $3-$5 million projects. Only one client has asked Matilda back for a project over $5 million.*

Matilda knew that Ling would likely quote many more statistics, but she thought the key ones she'd list-ed would be related to: 1) How long she'd been around. 2) How rarely she'd been invited back for projects that were bigger than the budget she'd gone in at. And final-ly, 3) How often she was asked back for even the small projects. He might even point out via cold hard numbers how she was not strategic, but either way, Matilda felt Ling would gather any and all evidence that supported his notion that she was not strategic. She cut the exer-cise a bit short too, convincing herself for the time being that at a certain point, the addition of one more data & status statement wouldn't make a difference.

Data & Status Case Study Wrap Up: You can see why Deck repeatedly told me he hated the Clarity Compass. Many people I work with feel overwhelmed by the level of frankness they have to negotiate with themselves throughout the Self and Other processes. But trust me that it's not all toil and trauma. As you begin to name and accept your mistakes and to gently readjust your Reality Maps, you move into a place of hope and even relief as the situations in your life begin to shift. On the other side of Deck and Matilda's frustration at stepping into the Other's shoes comes the acknowledgement that they can do it while continuing to move forward. The more patient and gentle you are with yourself as you walk your own journey, the more patient and gentle you can be with your Other.

Practicing Data & Status

Practicing data & status for the Other can be a little bit more idiosyncratic than for the other sub directions, meaning some people have an inclination for numbers where others have a penchant for job or position titles. Some people like to focus on dates and deadlines while others like to focus on financials. The key is to notice what's important to your Other. For this practice, you can think of any person and situation that comes to mind.

1. When the Other has tried to provide explanations or evidence in the past, what did you

notice them citing most frequently in terms of data & status?

2. As you continue to interact with this person, pay special attention to what data & status they tend to focus on and report. Notice if they pay attention at all to data & status. What *might* it mean if they don't?

Practicing Facts for Other

This completes our exploration of Facts for Other. Recall that when we work with Facts, the first step is to focus on observations rather than Stories and opinions. The next step is to reevaluate the criteria with which Facts are selected. And since the Facts that are selected usually build toward a case or Story, the third step is to notice what case is being built.

Going through the Facts process for ourselves is difficult enough, and it takes much more skill and mental acuity to go through this process as the Other—since we know they have a unique perspective. Developing empathetic guessing skills takes practice—there is no shortcut. As an end to this section then, let's take one more opportunity to practice.

1. Using an example from one of the other practices or a new situation, think about your Other's Facts. What does your Other directly know? Think of the video camera here—no judgment, just the Facts.

2. Which of the Facts (that your Other is aware of) are most relevant to the issue at hand according to the Other?

3. Follow up with your Other about the Facts. Be curious about the Facts that they are emphasizing.
4. Try to reach consensus on the important Facts.

Stories

Stories play an important role in creating meaning around the Facts we collect, the Intentions we pursue, and the Actions we take. The better we articulate our Stories, the more we are able to identify the contents of our Reality Maps. Now we will shift our perspective and look into the Stories of the Other so that we can piece together an appreciation of their Reality Maps.

When examining the Stories others may be living by, it is helpful to think about what they've said or done. Think for a second about your favorite fictional characters: How is it you relate to them as if they were real people?

The behaviors of a person—real or fictional—tend to be indicators of the beliefs they hold, as well as reflections of their inner experience. For example, if a person exercises for two hours every day, it is a reasonable assumption that they value fitness. Of course, we still need to be careful of thinking we know for sure what this person believes, because, like my client, Liam, it may be the case that they place little or no value on fitness, but exercise only to de-stress. Only if we have heard the other person state explicitly that they value fitness can we reason that it's highly likely that they genuinely value fitness. We make empathetic guesses as to the Stories people have based on the behaviors we observe in them, but there is no guarantee that the Stories we make up are accurate.

Now that we've chosen to think through the Facts that are important to the Other, it should be easier for us to sort through our Other's Stories. Their Stories are based, in part, on the Facts they choose to focus on, and this Facts vs. Stories combination should give you some insight into their Reality Maps.

Keep in mind that as you examine the Stories of your Other, you are likely to find inconsistencies and outright contradictions, but this process is not about finding things you disagree with and using that information to shame or hurt your Other. Constructive feedback can be helpful, but offering it is never about being right. Remember that you have your own Blind Spots and biases, and if you constantly correct your Other or confront their deep-seated beliefs, you risk reducing your effectiveness and damaging the relationship. Understanding where the Other is coming from is essential to engaging them in a Creative Conversation.

Much more important than correcting their Facts or shifting their Stories is the willingness to deeply understand their opinions and perspectives on these Facts and Stories. In this situation, empathetic guessing can result in benefits, such as the Other feeling heard, known, and appreciated, or in you realizing that there is more to their Story than you first thought. Occasionally too, they might wake up to the idea that some aspects of their thinking might be off.

Keep your "Big Challenge" in mind as you read through Stories for Other and the three associated sub directions: beliefs, emotions, and physiology.

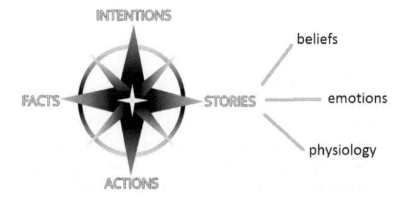

Beliefs

Recall that our Stories, and those of the Other, manifest, in part, in a variety of different types of beliefs. These beliefs range from conscious to unconscious, beneficial to harmful, stated to demonstrated, broad to specific, and from superficial to deep-rooted. In our efforts to understand the Reality Maps of Others, uncovering and exploring their beliefs plays a crucial role.

While your Other may have shared some of their beliefs with you over time, you will need to use empathetic guessing to get at those beliefs that are subtler and less frequently acknowledged. Interpersonal perspectives, such as your Other's opinion of you, or the way they think you see them, won't likely be stated aloud. Most people require a high level of trust before they'll reveal deeply personal beliefs.

Similarly, they may not mention any beliefs they consider irrelevant to their relationship with you or to the task at hand. Empathetic guessing is the best way to cast a wide net and expand the possibility of bringing hidden beliefs to light.

Let's see how Deck and Matilda go about this process.

DECK

Given his growing realization of how little he knew his employees, Deck was having self-doubts about his ability to access Lyle's beliefs. However, he also knew that even if his empathetic guessing was not one hundred percent accurate, it was moving him toward understanding Others in a way he had never been able to before. This encouraged him to take a stab at imagining what Lyle's beliefs were:

- ***Deck is very demanding.***
- ***Deck doesn't think people need help.***
- ***Deck doesn't tolerate imperfection well.***
- ***Deck will shout at me every time I screw up.***
- ***I feel unappreciated.***
- ***I feel that Deck doesn't see me as a person.***
- ***I feel like I'm screwing up all the time.***

As Deck looked at the words in front of him, he sensed a brief urge to rebel: *My employees may believe I'm like that, but I'm not! Maybe I have a short fuse, but is asking people to do their job properly such a terrible thing?*

He sat with this initial defensiveness of what he'd written, and then got back in touch with his shame. Maybe demanding the best of people was okay, but clearly he needed to do a lot more than *demand* it—he needed to somehow create an environment that would bring out the best in his employees. He re-examined his list and surrendered to the idea that it probably was reflective of his employees' thinking.

MATILDA

Matilda had spent so much time being angry at Ling that she hadn't really considered what he might believe about her. She used to have swim coaches though, who had been much more demanding, hadn't she? And she knew why those coaches operated the way they did. She thought quietly for a moment, then wrote (As Ling):

- *Matilda isn't invested in her future with the firm, so I shouldn't be invested in her.*
- *Matilda has not shown me any evidence that she thinks strategically.*
- *Matilda is a smart, dedicated worker, but she isn't fulfilling her potential.*
- *Matilda doesn't have kids and isn't married. If her personal life changes, any investment I make in her might be wasted.*
- *Matilda should ask me if there's anything else I need from her.*
- *Matilda should meet with me every week to review her projects.*
- *She can't deliver on the small tasks. What makes her think she can deliver on the larger tasks?*

Matilda didn't like this list. On the one hand, how dare Ling assume that she'd just stop working if her personal life changed? This belief might not be one Ling held, but Matilda was pretty sure it was part of the reason he showed so little confidence in her and had slammed her in reviews. Matilda gave an audible sigh. She wanted Ling to know that she was as dedicated to the firm and her future there as he was. She now had to figure out a way to communicate all this.

Beliefs for Other Case Study Wrap Up: Note that in the beliefs sub direction both Deck and Matilda experienced some negative reactivity—this is common in a contentious situation. When you truly step into the shoes of the Other, you will very likely find something that will trigger your defenses. But if you persevere (like Deck and Matilda) and continue to shed light on whatever uncomplimentary beliefs a person may have regarding you (and despite the fact you recognize that some of these beliefs might be valid), the rigidity of your Reality Maps will begin to loosen and your Blind Spots will shrink or become clearer.

As a final note, Deck is using the word "feel" in the beliefs sub direction, especially for those beliefs that seem vague or intuitive. We can also use the term "feel" in the emotion sub direction for statements that may contain beliefs, but have more of an emotional, visceral, or intuitive overtone. While for some the word "feeling" only connotes emotion, it is important to allow ourselves to use the word for subtle, somatic, or intuitive experiences where we're not yet able to label it clearly as an emotion or belief.

Practicing Beliefs for Other

Let's now explore the beliefs of your Other. Think of a situation where you and another person share a difference of opinion. Remember to be as objective as you can and try to feel into what they might be thinking or feeling.

1. Try to step into the other person's perspective by examining the values they seem to hold and operate by. What long-term beliefs do you imagine they have that could be broad or deep-seated, or both?
2. You don't need to come to an agreement with the Other, but try to see that based on the broader context of the world that their Reality Maps provide, it makes some sense that they have their perspective in this situation.

If you are really struggling to see how your Other's perspective makes sense, you may want to share your desire to understand their point of view and engage in a dialogue with them—not to convince them of your views, but to more deeply explore their Reality Maps and better understand the context from which they are operating.

Remember that the main benefit and tool in stepping into the Other's perspective is curiosity. If better understanding and effectiveness follow this exercise, great—if not, accept limitations and move on.

Emotions

As we discussed in the Clarity Compass for Self, emotions play a unique role in the creation of our Stories. In fact, our emotional responses, in many ways, are the glue of our Reality Maps—they hold our Maps together and make certain dimensions of our Stories very "sticky," or hard to let go of.

I hope that you were able to discover a lot about your own deeply held perspectives and emotions when you worked through the exercises for Self. Now we will build on that understanding through the much more challenging task of exploring the emotional terrain of our Other's stories, with the hopes of more clearly understanding why they do the things they do.

Recall that emotions serve a variety of functions, guiding everything from basic everyday communications to the expression of the depths of our soul. Most of our emotions are derivations or combinations of the four primary emotions: sad, mad, glad, and afraid. We sometimes refer to our emotions as feelings, but feelings can also encompass all of our felt senses. Emotions influence our biases, judgments, and predispositions.

The opportunity for you now is to perceive how your Other's emotions impact them. As always, unless they go out of their way to explain their emotions to you, there is no way for you to uncover and know for sure any or all of your Other's emotions. So, once again, we employ empathetic guessing based on their behavior or external appearance. Given the same situation, if you were in the Other's shoes, how might you feel? Given the deeper wants you have imagined for them, what might they be feeling given the outcomes they've received?

One of the best ways to determine the emotions of the Other is to observe their behavior or physiology. Have you noticed their face flushing, sweat, or tension in their jaw? Did their voice become softer or did the tone of their voice shift? Body language carries powerful messages: Your Other might move slightly closer or further away from you, cross their arms, or look you more intensely in the eye. Their gestures might become more grandiose or passive. The point in mentioning their behaviors and physiology in this emotions section is that you are an investigator looking for clues to indicate what emotions a person may be having.

Careful observation with empathetic guessing is the best way to understand the emotions and feelings of your Other without asking them about their emotions directly. I remember one participant in a Clarity Compass program who, after completing an exercise, said, "When I put myself in the place of the other person and began to see how they saw me and to feel what they were likely feeling, I started to hate myself."

While I'm clearly not encouraging you to have negative feelings toward yourself, I do encourage you to step into the other person's perspective so powerfully that you experience how they might be experiencing the situation and you. While your Other may not feel resentment or frustration toward you in general, it is typical for them to hold negative or unpleasant feelings in situations where there is significant disagreement. The point in this exercise is to try to fully experience the unique flavor of the Other's emotional experience. Doing so will allow you to develop more empathy for them, and will clear the way toward making a difference or transforming.

Now let's see how Deck and Matilda confronted this challenge.

DECK

For Deck, looking at his own emotions had been very difficult, so he was hesitant about trying to step into the emotions of another person. Still, he felt a sense of pride in regards to his self-revelations thus far, so he wrote (as Lyle):

- ***I feel frustrated.***
- ***I feel sad.***

- ***I feel hurt.***
- ***I feel angry.***
- ***I feel hopeless.***
- ***I feel trapped (panicky, frustrated).***

This list of feelings made Deck sad. Obviously, people screw up from time to time and he shouldn't scream at them over minor mistakes. No self-respecting, competent person should have to tolerate being treated with as little respect as Deck had often shown. People were leaving in droves because of him. If he wanted to change things for his company, he'd have to change himself first.

Deck looked back at his first Clarity Compass entry—a scope that encompassed working out why his people were leaving. He'd solved that question, but there was a lot left to explore. By now, Deck understood that the Clarity Compass was a fluid tool, so he scratched out the old scope and wrote:

Scope: *I need to find the best ways to change, so my people will stay.*

MATILDA

Matilda faced the emotions section with a heavy heart. Her failures were so clear to her now and she had so much work to do that she almost didn't care how Ling felt about her. All she really wanted to do was book a ticket straight to Hawaii and spend ten days playing in the surf. But she knew she had to stay put and list each of the emotions she imagined for Ling, along with a related belief. She wrote (as Ling):

- *I feel <u>frustrated</u> that I can't seem to bring Matilda up to the performance level I need her to meet.*
- *I feel <u>worried</u> that if the firm keeps carrying non-performing executives, we might wind up in financial trouble.*
- *I feel <u>anxious</u> about the decisions I've made investing in Matilda so far, when it might have been for nothing.*
- *I feel <u>embarrassed</u> that she works for me and is not performing to the standards that she should be.*

In realizing how much emotional distress she might be causing Ling, Matilda found it difficult to stay present. She sat with her findings for a while, but then wanted to quickly go to Action. She didn't want to continue to let Ling down. She would improve.

In thinking about Ling's emotions, Matilda was able to see him in a much more empathetic light, which helped her feel more forgiving of him, which in turn, oddly, pulled a weight off her shoulders. All of a sudden, her problem wasn't that some unreasonable person she couldn't control was intentionally hindering her progress. She knew she had to take charge of herself and complete certain tasks and projects in order to change Ling's view of her. Everything she needed to do to be made a senior partner was under her control.

Now of course, this realization prompted new questions: Why hadn't she already done what was necessary to be promoted? What, specifically, was stopping her?

Clearly, she would have to take an additional round with the Clarity Compass using a new scope not just to resolve becoming more strategic, but to resolve her lack of compliance with Ling's assignments.

Emotions for Other Case Study Wrap Up: At this point, both Deck and Matilda have both tangibly adjusted their scopes. As you go through your Clarity Compasses—for Self or for Other—you may revise earlier entries or add a whole new Clarity Compass to the mix. The more Clarity Compasses you do, the more you will know when one is enough and when you'll have to do a little editing and adding.

So again, in tracking the totality of Deck's progress, you see that the problem of his scope evolved from "people are leaving" and the notion that it was their fault to "people are leaving for justified reasons," to "people are leaving and it may be due to me," and finally, to "I'm driving people away and I need to change." Sticking to his progress on his original Clarity Compass though, here's what we see:

When Deck wrote (as Lyle), "I feel trapped," he was actually writing out a belief, but nevertheless it was what Deck had imagined as for Lyle—it was an emotional experience akin to desperation or panic that he thought Lyle was having a difficult time expressing.

Matilda mixed her beliefs sub direction in with her emotions sub direction, in part because she saw Ling's beliefs as causing his emotions (i.e. his frustration, worry, and anxiety). As I noted earlier, combining these two sub directions is fine as long as it doesn't distract from a focus on emotions, and as long as it challenges the beliefs that are questionable. For example, Matilda wrote as Ling that she was "a nonperforming executive," but this was not the case at all. At the project delivery level, she was one of the highest-performing executives in the firm, she just had less of an impact on strategy. She may imagine that Ling believes her to be a non-performer, but she should then also include that belief in the beliefs sub direction. Here, mentioning the belief in the emotions sub direction is fine since it helped her get to the frustration, worry, and anxiety that she imagines Ling having.

Practicing Emotions for the Other

Since you've already thought through your "Big Challenge," think of another challenging situation you've been working with.

1. What deeper wants do you believe the Other has?
2. What Facts (including their specific Actions and other behaviors) and Stories do you believe they have?
3. Given what you list in Steps One and Two, if you were the Other, what emotions would you likely have?
4. Just as your Stories create your disposition, the Other's disposition is a reflection of their Story. Let go of your disposition as much as you can in order to step more deeply into theirs and to sense how they would be feeling. Take the time to really feel and name whatever emotions come up when you have placed yourself into the Other's perspective. As you step more deeply into their story and disposition, what emotions and emotionally laden beliefs might they be having?

Physiology

With the physiology sub direction, we are once again imagining the internal experience of the Other, but rather than focusing on their emotional experience, we're looking at their experience through their body. We are trying to notice where, as the Other, we feel tense, relaxed, sore, tired, achy, etc. These physical cues can give us insight into the world of the Other and, as with all aspects of the Clarity Compass for Other, help us to gain and share more empathy and understanding. Because this sub direction is usually the most difficult of all the Clarity Compass sub directions, some people understandably try to skip it. But taking a moment to imagine what someone else might be feeling inside their own skin is valuable, and for this step especially, I urge clients not to worry too much about the accuracy of their empathetic guesses. This sub direction for Other is almost impossible to "get at," because essentially, you are imagining what it is like to physically be someone else—what is it like not just to be in their shoes, but in their skin?

All we can ever do is our best—and Deck and Matilda were troopers in this regard. Let's see how they went about completing this sub direction.

DECK

Deck resisted completing the physiology sub direction because, like many of my clients, he thought it would be a waste of time. "But hey," he said, "I know I've balked a few times throughout this process and have wound up with some really interesting insights, so, here goes nothing!" He went ahead and wrote (as Lyle):

- *When Deck yells at me, I feel myself get red-faced.*
- *My stomach tightens whenever I get an email from Deck*
- *My voice gets softer when Deck is around.*
- *When Deck starts to lean forward I feel myself pull back.*
- *Since Deck is a big, muscular guy, I try not to get too close to him.*
- *Sometimes I can't sleep at night.*

While Deck made up most of the above—he couldn't know about Lyle's sleeping habits, for example—he had witnessed a number of these physiological responses, such as Lyle turning red and keeping his distance. Now that he was confronting this information more directly in the context of the Clarity Compass, it helped him complete the picture of what it might have been like for Lyle to have worked under him.

MATILDA

Because of her years in competitive swimming, Matilda considered herself a fairly astute observer of the physiology of others.

As Ling, she wrote:

- *I feel exhausted from all of my hours of work.*
- *I feel stressed every time I think of Matilda.*
- *I feel tension in my head.*

With the number of hours that Ling worked, it made sense to Matilda that he would be exhausted. It didn't seem like much of a leap either to guess that she caused him stress, given the number of times he had criticized her lack of performance, and the idea that he probably held himself fully accountable for her performance. As for the headaches, Matilda had them too, so it wasn't much of a stretch to assume Ling would have them. Even if he didn't hold tension in his head, he likely felt it somewhere.

Either way, as Matilda played with possible physical experiences Ling might be having, she was surprised at how much compassion was welling up in her. She could feel herself hoping that Ling would get some rest. She had truly come a long way!

Physiology for Other Case Study Wrap Up: Both Deck and Matilda used their observational powers to guess the physiology of their Other. While this physiology exercise is rarely earth shattering, by working through it, both Deck and Matilda enhanced the picture they were creating of their Other.

Practicing Physiology for the Other

As I mentioned, some people find it difficult or pointless to imagine what another person might be feeling in their body, but others find it meaningful and fun. See what happens for you as you practice imagining what another person might be experiencing in their body. Assuming you've been practicing the physiology sub direction with your "Big Challenge" already, think of a person you know fairly well.

1. Write down everything you can think of regarding the Other's physical presence. Think about their

posture, depth of breath, voice pitch, tone, cadence, how they walk, the gestures they make, and their way of dressing. Jot down a couple of key comments or phrases they tend to make. What are their tics?

2. Find some privacy and space so you can physically "test" everything you listed. As best you can, take on the Other's posture and rate of breathing. Say aloud a couple of phrases they tend to use, repeating yourself "as the Other" several times, until you get their pitch, tone, cadence, and gestures right.

3. Stay with this exercise for a few minutes, taking on as many of the Other's characteristics as you can, until you've imagined them as fully and completely as possible. If it helps, try taking on some of the thoughts and beliefs they have under their Stories. Allow yourself to imagine being this other person as fully and completely as you can.

Practicing Stories for Other

While the Stories sub directions are helpful reference points, don't spend too much time trying to discern which sub direction a thought goes into. The important thing is to get as many relevant thoughts, emotions, and physiological traits down on paper as possible. For example, if you're not sure whether something would be more an emotion or a belief for the Other, use the term "feeling" followed by whatever possible emotion or belief you are sensing. I'm saving the word "feelings" for these visceral, intuitive vague senses that don't seem to be clear "beliefs" or "emotions." Clearly labeling whether a statement is a belief or emotion can be liberating, but having an Ego driven demand for this level of control and definition often cuts us off from subtler ambiguous senses that only the Heart can understand. The Clarity Compass seeks to categorize along directions and sub directions, but is always flexible, agile, and accommodating.

Take a moment to reflect on the challenges you encountered during your immersion in the Stories for Other direction. You can continue to practice and grow your empathy by weaving together and practicing everything you've explored thus far. Assuming you've already been contemplating your "Big Challenge" for this practice, consider a different situation.

1. Think about your Other's Facts. What does your Other not know, meaning, what can they therefore only guess at?
2. What does their worldview prompt them to think about the situation?
3. Writing Practice:
   a. As the Other, write out the things they believe.
   b. As the Other, write out their emotions.
   c. As the Other, write out your best guess of what their body is feeling.
   d. Attempt to pull together their beliefs, emotions, and physiology by actively thinking their thoughts, feeling their emotions and sensing what it's like to be in their body. Breathe into this experience, allowing yourself to become them as much as it is empathetically possible.

Summary of Facts Versus Stories Polarity

We started the Facts vs. Stories polarity by first exploring what Facts might be important to the Other and how they might be using those Facts to build their Stories. On one hand, we are always trying to distinguish Facts from Stories, but at the very same time, we acknowledge that a dynamic relationship exists between the two elements. We separate Stories from Facts, but we also recognize that the greater the number of Facts that are closely related to a Story, the greater the likelihood the Story is true. Finally, a Story is never a Fact, but a Story can have degrees of truth to it.

We know now also that the Facts we choose to focus on aren't necessarily the same others choose. Furthermore, we may not have the same access to the same Facts, and we might accidentally overlook or purposefully ignore a Fact that our Other thinks is essential (and vice versa). Being open to this kind of ebb and flow of information, while still encouraging its exchange, is essential to building stronger relationships and clearer lines of communication.

In the Stories section we used empathetic guessing to gain insight into how our Other responds to the Facts that *they* have, which lets us further imagine their Reality Maps and what they might be seeing and not seeing thanks to their Blind Spots. There is a degree to which it is possible for us to predict which Facts our Other will use to support their opinions, allowing us to discern their Intentions and thereby imagine what Actions they will take. We explored the ways in which our Other's Reality Maps are influenced by a set of beliefs, emotions, and physiological traits that may differ vastly, or hardly at all, from our own. Of course, even as we develop and practice our empathetic guessing skills over time, we will never be right or accurate about the Other all the time—we shouldn't even aim for this. But movement towards empathetically experiencing the Other's reality is essential for our growth, transformation, and effectiveness, as well as theirs and that of the larger community.

Now that we have completed our exploration of the Facts vs. Stories Polarity for Other, it is time to circle back, as we did for the Self section and circumnavigate our Clarity Compass for Self and Other.

CHAPTER 4

Circumnavigation

By now, you may be feeling pretty strong in your understanding of the Clarity Compass, both for Self and Other. We've worked through each of the Polarities, Directions, and sub directions in much depth, so you might feel that you're ready to move into Action. I understand how tempting it is to feel "complete" and "ready to roll." However, you still have one final step, which is actually the most important part of your journey thus far. I call it circumnavigation.

Circumnavigation is the practice of stepping back and using the Clarity Compass to see your situation more holistically. While for most of the book, we've been exploring each of its component parts step-by-step, the Clarity Compass is, in essence, a completely interrelated whole. Each sub direction is intimately related to all the other sub directions, and circumnavigation is essentially reviewing everything you've done so far in an effort to illuminate the often hidden connections between the many seemingly disparate insights you've had thus far. At first, this may seem redundant because you've already naturally begun to see the many ways that each sub direction is related to the others as you've worked through your Clarity Compass in the previous chapters. However, by stepping back from the process entirely you'll experience a broader vantage point where you are able to see how all the pieces fit together as a whole. Circumnavigation is the final step before moving into Action, and is an especially crucial aspect of preparing for Creative Conversations.

Let's use a simple example to explore the practice of circumnavigating your Clarity Compass. You and your business partner Marybeth are considering a new venture. The venture was your idea (your desired outcome) and you are using the Clarity Compass to make sure that both of you are on the same page moving forward. You've identified that she has a deeper want for financial security and you know that the outcomes you are seeking around the new venture would create financial risk for her. As you circumnavigate, you would further explore what emotions might come up for her around that deeper want for security: frustration, disappointment, or even fear. Next, you may notice that you need to write more about her beliefs in order to understand why security is so important to her and what it might look like. Perhaps she has a belief around the importance of reducing chaos and increasing control?

Circumnavigation can often be similar to detective work: looking for clues and then trying to figure out what each of them means. For example, you can sometimes notice the emotions that your Other is experiencing in a given situation, and from there, can imagine what outcome they were seeking that would cause those emotions. If you wrote that the person was sad or disappointed, you might explore the possibility that they had a desire for achieving a particular goal that wasn't met or for a particular situation to be different. The source of sadness, then, is an unmet or unwanted desire—a very common thing!

This circumnavigation section may seem redundant because rather than introducing a new direction or sub direction, we're using the Clarity Compass terminology you've already learned and highlighting how one term relates to the other. But this is really where all the action is. We're *applying* everything we've learned and weaving together a cohesive picture of the situation so we can move into action.

Let's explore another example of circumnavigation. This time with a mundane incident that we've all probably experienced at one time or another: You are troubled that a friend is not calling you back. The problem statement in the scope is that you want your friend to return your call but, for whatever reason, they aren't.

You could explore the emotions this situation is bringing up for you, possibly frustration and a feeling of rejection. You could then explore what deeper want might be dwelling beneath these emotions and your desire for the call back. You may find that you have a deeper want for a sense of community, or for simply feeling valued and respected. So then what beliefs in your Reality Maps are creating your current experience? The said & done is that you called your friend a number of times and the not done is that your friend has not yet called back. Now what Stories are surrounding these Facts? What Stories do you have around the protocol of making and returning phone calls? How do you define community and measure feeling valued?

In this case, you can see that we have focused solely on how your friend's Actions (or in this case, lack of action) have impacted the sub directions as they relate to your Self. But you now also have the skills to extend the Clarity Compass to Other, so you can begin to explore what Stories your friend may have around the etiquette of taking and returning (repeat) phone calls.

By circumnavigating the Clarity Compass for Other, we are filling in many gaps in our understanding of the internal landscape of the other person. For example, we might ask what the Facts are in their history of returning calls. I have friends who take days or sometimes weeks to return personal calls, whereas other friends call back within hours. In the former case, I begin to make up all kinds of Stories—from the mild to the inane—as to why they haven't called back. Why aren't they meeting my expectations? Do they have any clue what my expectations are?

Unlike the Clarity Compass we did earlier in the book where we worked sequentially in the order of the Four Directions, circumnavigation is a more organic process where we follow the logical threads of how each of the sub directions naturally relates to the others. The end goal is to have a comprehensive picture of what *might* be going on with your friend and what is *likely* going on for you as far as your self-awareness can take you. From this place, the hope is that you will not only be able to more easily manage your experience moving forward, but will also be able to define and select the most effective leveraged Actions for the situation at hand. In this case, circumnavigating for Self helps you to be more emotionally intelligent through refining your understanding of the situation and working with your own beliefs and emotions. You begin to loosen your attachment to your friend calling back, as well as have fewer assumptions about the possibilities as to why they have not. Depending on the situation with your friend, you may end up making a specific request that they give you a quick call or text to let you know they are okay. Alternatively, it might be best to think about meeting up with other crucial friends to satisfy your deeper want for connection. Your specific, leveraged Action step will correlate directly with the result of your circumnavigating your Clarity Compass for Self and Other.

For any situation, from the mundane to the significant, after having completed all of the sub directions for Self and Other, you will want to circumnavigate in order to fill in any remaining gaps, and to ensure there is as much congruence as possible amongst all of the sub directions. Compare one sub direction with the others—looking for interrelated clues, insights, and patterns. Then, and this is often the most important step, pull back the camera lens so that you can take in the most all-encompassing Reality Map of the situation.

Taking this final step—circumnavigation—cues our imagination to think even more deeply about Self and Other and to come up with insights that were not readily available the first time(s) we worked through the Clarity Compass. Once we complete the circumnavigation for Self and Other, we are more prepared to revisit the Actions Direction to determine the next best step.

This practice occurs to some people as tedious, but with practice you will be able to intuitively move through your Clarity Compass to see where the most critical relationships within your Reality Maps reside. Other people find the practice of circumnavigating as relaxing and grounding. They find themselves able to pull out of the details and see the interconnections within a more global picture.

We'll see now in our case studies how circumnavigating enabled Deck and Matilda to get a better understanding of the situation—which is crucial—prior to planning their Creative Conversations.

DECK

As I was sitting with Deck, he began looking over his answers for the Clarity Compass for Self and Other and to circumnavigate through everything he'd written. As he reviewed his deeper wants, it hit him that while his two needs for control and prosperity had at first seemed mutually supporting of each other, he was now starting to see that his deeper want for control also caused him to overly control people. This was creating an atmosphere of chaos—that was clear, based on the Facts of his high turnover rate—which did not support his prosperity.

He also realized that there was nothing in his own deeper wants around the need for belonging or connecting at work. He was fine having those needs met solely in his personal life. It hit him that just because this wasn't his deeper want, didn't mean other people didn't have it. He sighed. "Look at all this muck the Clarity Compass dredges up!" he said. And repeated, "I hate the Clarity Compass!"

But Deck continued to circumnavigate and because he took this time to step back, it became increasingly clear that:

- ***His lack of positive engagement was actually rendering him less in control, diminishing his prosperity, and making him less at ease.***
- ***His abrasiveness had a far bigger impact on others and on the company than he realized.***

- ***His disinterest in others beyond what they could do for him was far more damaging than he had realized. He and his employees were negatively impacted by his lack of empathy and curiosity.***
- ***He was emotionally frustrated and frequently visited by bouts of dread.***
- ***He would have to change.***

Deck hated the Clarity Compass alright, but at the same time, he could sense his Reality Maps shifting and could feel himself preparing to behave in ways that went against his own grain. He knew that he had a deep and broad belief that socializing at work was a waste of time, and that he was going to have to wrestle with this belief every time he had a "touchy-feely" conversation. He checked in with his body and was confused when he wrote, "I feel a bit sick to my stomach, but can feel my shoulders beginning to relax." A basic, military training image popped into his mind: He was trying to scale a 30-foot wall. He was exhausted, his fingers bloodied. Suddenly, he saw another soldier to his right, down on one knee creating a stirrup in his hands for Deck to step into.

Something deep had shifted in Deck. He went back to his beliefs and wrote, "People are a worthwhile investment." He slowly put his pen down and simply walked out of the room.

He was done circumnavigating for now.

MATILDA

Matilda wanted some privacy for her circumnavigation, so she worked through her Clarity Compass while she was home by herself. She reported the following highlights to me:

"I once again read through all that I had written. I came back to my Clarity Compass for Other and could easily see the bigger picture from Ling's perspective." She listed the following insights:

- *I added a bit more in his deeper wants: (as Ling) "I want to feel at peace with having worked hard and accomplished much."*
- *I added to his outcomes: (as Ling) "I want Matilda to perform well and to demonstrate that she's earned senior partner status."*
- *I added his situational wants: (as Ling) "I want Matilda's performance to reflect well on me."*
- *I went back to his beliefs: (as Ling) "Matilda is an embarrassment for me."*

Working through Ling as Other made her feel sick to her stomach and she cried (her physiology). So she began to circumnavigate her Self.

- *I went back to my emotions: "I hate Ling."*
- *I returned to my emotions: "I still hate Ling."*
- *I went to my deeper wants: "I do want to feel successful and competent."*
- *My beliefs: "Ling makes me feel unsuccessful and incompetent."*

Matilda continued to speak: "Having vented and allowed myself to fully step into hating and blaming Ling, I felt like I created room for myself to figure out a way to name and meet my deeper wants, in order to let them go. I soon realized though that letting them go was not an option yet, because they were so deeply ingrained. So I settled on the pursuit of simply trying to figure out and meet my deeper wants. I realized I couldn't do it all at once, and would have to be patient with my transformation. I had gained the skills and confidence to make it happen, I just had to slow my pace and give myself kudos for recognizing even that need. In terms of my beliefs: I confess I could be more strategic and responsive to Ling."

"I was planning on spending more time circumnavigating, but as soon as I wrote my last belief, I could feel that was the focus. I realize that I could keep defending myself and making Ling wrong, and I probably will slip back into this pattern from time to time. But in the end, if I don't accept that I need to make some significant changes in and for myself, with or without regards to Ling, I'm going to be stuck on the same treadmill forever."

Circumnavigation for Other Case Study Wrap Up: Through the process of circumnavigating, both Deck and Matilda not only began to see their situations differently, but they also began to see themselves in the world differently—that is, they began to personally transform.

They each took responsibility for their Blind Spots, and could see more powerfully than ever where they were creating or co-creating misery in their own lives and in the lives of others. By examining how each of the sub directions wove together, their Reality Maps began to unravel, shift, and reform into new Stories. While each experienced a painful realization about their contributions to the negative situations at hand, this realization ultimately brought about a new freedom. This new freedom, in turn, lit their imaginations and generated opportunities for novel behaviors and new ways of engaging.

It's likely that not all of your Clarity Compass work will be as painful or revelatory as Deck and Matilda's, but the greater your willingness to circumnavigate with scrutiny, the greater the likelihood that a new Story with fresh and unforeseen possibilities for you and others around you will emerge.

CHAPTER **5**

Creative Conversations

As social beings, we create our lives through conversations. If we want to have a more effective and harmonious life, we need to examine and upgrade the kinds of interactions that we are having. While the Clarity Compass is designed first to help us examine and evolve our thinking, the ultimate goal is to improve our interactions with others, particularly through having more Creative Conversations. These conversations are infused with respect, curiosity, collaboration, imagination, and possibility.

In the Self section, we focused on examining your own perspective going into Creative Conversations. In this chapter, we'll focus on an equally important aspect of preparing for and engaging in a Creative Conversation: stepping into the shoes of the Other. Now that you've worked through the Clarity Compass for Other, you've seen that the Other lives in a completely different reality. Their Reality Maps and Blind Spots are likely quite different from your own and in order to have Creative Conversations with others, it's crucial that we make the effort to see the world through their eyes. Once we have this clarity, we can powerfully move forward in the interaction.

Of course, focusing on the Other doesn't mean absolving yourself of responsibility in a conversation.

Remember the old cliché, "If it's meant to be, it's up to me." I see my clients make this mistake all the time: as we start to focus on the Other, they tend to feel like they're off the hook. But while the other person does have responsibility in the conversation, the more we expect them to resolve the situation the less inclined we are to take responsibility for the success of the conversation.

Understanding your own responsibility for a conversation is most important in situations when it seems that the Other doesn't seem willing to cooperate. It is still possible to work toward having a Creative Conversation by stepping further into the Other's shoes and seeing what they are wanting. In circumstances such as these, you will have to hold yourself even more responsible for the outcome of the situation. Yes—I understand—the latter part of that sentence, "you will have to hold yourself even more responsible for the outcome of the situation," is disturbing for most people. Wouldn't it be much easier to set our sights on the other person's lack of cooperation, and complain? Sometimes, it feels easier to throw our hands in the air and give up, or to stay stuck. But it is crucial that you find the wherewithal to draw upon your Clarity Compass toolkit and move the situation forward. This is not a position of self-blame, but a position of self-empowerment. In the end, we may not get anything close to what we want and the other person may remain uncooperative; however, the greatest likelihood of success rests in our taking responsibility and using the Clarity Compass to do the best we can and having a Creative Conversation.

Time and time again, I've seen my clients (and myself) underestimate their own responsibility in moving a conversation forward, or backward. Let's use one of my favorite conversation metaphors to illuminate this point: that of a dance between yourself and the Other. Picture your conversation to be a discombobulated ballroom dance in which both you and your dance partner (the Other) are out of sync with each other. Imagine that your partner is a less capable dancer than yourself and causing much of the discombobulation. If you were to respond to the situation by simply doing the same thing and waiting for your dance partner to get with the program, the likelihood is that your dance will continue to look similarly bad. However, if you were to shift to the Charleston or some nifty improvisational jazz, it will be difficult for your dance partner to continue your awkward ballroom dancing patterns. Remember, the only way to get different results is to engage in different behaviors. Of course, taking full responsibility for a conversation your Other isn't willing to help you out with doesn't mean you're to blame if things don't change or turn out well. It simply means that you hold yourself accountable in the continued march toward imagining new and creative ways of engaging.

But again, let's consider the best of circumstances: You have prepared for a Creative Conversation by stepping into the shoes of the Other, so you can better understand where they are coming from, and gradually you do learn what they want out of the exchange—you see too what might be keeping the situation from moving forward. Ideally, you have completed a Clarity Compass for both the Self and Other. Of course, there will be many instances in which you can't prepare for a Creative Conversation ahead of time. You won't necessarily have time to do your empathetic guesses before you engage. But stepping into the Other's shoes is something you can also do mid-conversation.

Also, in examining the requests sub directions for Self, we discussed making the requests compelling. Now that you have completed your Clarity Compass for Other, you will better be able to make the request that you're making of your Other compelling based on knowing their deeper wants and understanding what's meaningful to them. Make sure that you include your compelling requests within your Creative Conversations.

Finally, there are two more powerful concepts that you can explore during Creative Conversations: Being Curious and Mirroring.

Being Curious

Cultivating curiosity within a conversation is one of the most critical skills to practice as we are having a Creative Conversation with our Other, but sadly, most of the leaders I work with are more invested in providing great answers than in being curious about the Other. Most leaders can't help it; every time they provide a great answer they are in fact strongly reinforced, so their habit of contributing through telling becomes more and more deeply embedded. One of my favorite aspects of what I do entails the undoing of these habits. Curiosity, I explain to clients who are stuck, helps us shift from a "telling" or informing disposition to a listening disposition. This shift in roles and perspectives frees us to learn and grow. Ask about his or her experience, situation, and hopes.

Most people I work with do see themselves as good listeners—whether they are CEOs, mid-level managers, or entry level employees. Many take pride in their listening skills, but everyone can improve how deeply they listen and how much they take in. This next section on mirroring is an invitation to be open to the possibility that you can listen far more powerfully than you currently do. Practice listening more intently to the subtleties of what others are saying. I invite you now to begin to explore what quantum leaps in listening are available!

Mirroring

Another way to develop a Creative Conversation is through the process of mirroring. Mirroring is a form of paraphrasing mixed with empathetic guessing where you describe how you are experiencing and understanding the other person during your conversation. It can be used to reflect gifts, deficiencies, orientations, dispositions, values, and so on. For example, I might say to an Other, "I can't help but notice that you seem upset about something. Is there something bothering you that we need to address?" We like to think we already know who we are and what life is about, but we know we don't. When done well, mirroring provides the other person with a powerful sense of being heard. It gives them insight into who they are by reflecting not only what they have said, but also how they are coming across to you.

Levels of Paraphrasing

When I talk about mirroring, I don't mean simply parroting someone's exact words. Here are some examples of how you might respond to someone, moving from simple parroting to mirroring. If the other person in your conversation says, **"I'm really tired. I hired a consultant**

to manage my marketing, but now I have to do everything myself at the last minute." You might say:

1. You're tired, huh?
2. You're really tired, since you hired a consultant to manage your marketing and now have to do everything yourself at the last minute.
3. You're really tired since you have had to do all of this last minute marketing work that you had hired a marketing consultant to do.
4. You sound tired and frustrated by having to do extra work that you already paid someone else to do.
5. It seems like this marketing consultant took advantage of you by taking your money and actually leaving you more work to do than before, which has left you feeling exhausted and let down.

Note the progression from simply (and somewhat thoughtlessly) repeating what your conversation partner just said, to adding a deeper level of understanding and compassion. The first example merely parrots the Other's tiredness and misses entirely their mention of the marketing consultant.

The second statement includes the "marketing consultant," but basically just repeats exactly what the Other said without demonstrating any real effort to understand where they are coming from. Some might even respond, "Yeah, that's what I just said." The only time I parrot like this is if someone says something particularly complex that I am repeating back more for my benefit than for theirs, or when someone says something that sounds like their careful wording has particular meaning for them.

The third statement uses the Other's words, but in a different order. It therefore reflects some higher level of listening, but is still not much deeper an effort than the prior statement.

Statement #4 paraphrases in a summary. Notice that the marketing function is left out, since it does not seem key to the listener. What is emphasized and mirrored back is the tired (said) from extra work (not said) as well as the frustration (not said) about extra work (not said). All of the "not said" came about thanks to reasonable empathetic guessing. Most people, if they heard this type of mirroring, would feel like their conversation partner had taken some time to truly listen and empathize with them. Typically, the speaker would then either correct one of the assumptions if it was off, or would feel heard and be encouraged to expound on some portion of what they just said. They might say, for example, "That's the last time I pay somebody completely in advance," or "Yeah, I could really use some rest."

The last paraphrase, #5, is the greatest leap, and takes a lot of practice to pull off. The Other may not be upset or thinking the other person took advantage of them, but if you are paying special attention to their tone of voice, you may want to reach out and share what you see or sense. If you are right, the Other will likely feel heard and possibly wake up to the sense they were feeling that way. Your empathy may help push them to realize the need to take care of themselves better physically or financially. It might create the space for them to realize that they are feeling like a victim and need to snap out of it or take further Action to rectify the situation. If you are incorrect in your assumptions, no worries! The Other can easily explain what they are experiencing to correct the piece that was off.

Sure, there is risk in mirroring: The further the empathetic guess is from the Facts of what the Other said, the greater the likelihood that it's off. But the more you practice mirroring, the better you become at it and the more impactful your conversations become.

I use mirroring around fifty percent of the time, during leadership coaching sessions. It usually results in clients not only feeling heard, but more importantly, it helps them to evolve their own way of thinking. As I name their behaviors and statements and hold them up for them to reflect upon, I watch as their thinking at first breaks apart, and then comes back together in a clearer, more cohesive fashion. It may seem like this process requires more time than simply letting people know they are "wrong" or telling them what to do, but I've found that people are less defensive and more open to changing and moving into action if given the opportunity to reflect deeply and with Intention.

It's true that most mirroring is empathetic and positive, so mirroring may sound like an overly gentle approach, but inevitably a majority of my clients respond to some of my paraphrasing by saying, "It sounds so much worse when I hear it from you."

Not that I enjoy giving clients negative feedback, I don't—the goal of mirroring is never to be judgmental, manipulative, or harsh. When mirroring, you should try to avoid putting in your own personal agenda. But again, good mirroring brings people a more thorough understanding of their Reality Maps and their way of expressing themselves. Those moments when my clients discover an inconsistency in their worldview provide windows for them to work on rethinking their situations and their lives.

It's easy for people to get defensive around their Reality Maps, so you may want to stick to simple paraphrasing at first and slowly extend your empathetic guessing within the conversation toward your subtler observations and assumptions. Mirroring is a skill that takes time to develop, but it is much more influential than simply giving someone advice.

Excellent mirroring comes from deep listening and as we become better listeners, we learn not to mirror everything back that we hear or assume. Through our empathetic listening, we want to determine the kind of communication style the Other prefers. For example: written versus oral, spontaneous versus advanced notice, in-person versus via phone, fast-paced versus slow-paced, here & now versus there and then, close physical proximity versus more distance, conceptually based versus data-based, and personal versus formal. The list is endless.

Your job is to be curious enough about others to notice their "go-to" communication styles and to figure out which communication styles you can use to make the most positive impact on them. Sometimes, how a person speaks can vary greatly from how they prefer to be spoken to. For example, Dave may love to speak in terms of Stories, but may be most influenced by Facts. This whole book is about seeing important nuances within yourself, as well as within the Other. Learning the nuances of the other person's preferred communication styles is an important step in becoming more discerning about the Other.

When and How Creative Conversations Go Wrong

Every so often a client comes back to me, lamenting that the Creative Conversation they had spent so much time preparing for did not result in the outcome they wanted. The fact is that people are complex and challenging. A Creative Conversation is not a magic wand you can wave over a person and instantly get everything you've ever wanted. Creative Conversations are a dynamic tool designed to help you build relationships that benefit both parties. It may not always go perfectly, but I believe that by using Creative Conversations (and the Clarity Compass in general) you're using *the best possible tools to create the greatest likelihood for the best outcomes*. While we cannot hope to have perfect conversations every single time with every single person we encounter, with practice, we become more fluid and highly impactful using the Clarity Compass for Creative Conversations.

Creative Conversations with Deck and Matilda

Now let's look at how Deck and Matilda approached their Creative Conversations. As you review their conversations, note how much progress each of them has made in terms of emotional intelligence and openness to the process.

DECK

Although armed with a deepening realization that his abrasiveness and disinterest towards his employees was at the root of why so many of them were leaving him,

Deck's Creative Conversation happened suddenly, so he had no time to prepare.

Only a few days after he had decided to come up with a game plan for treating his employees differently, a woman named Esme knocked on his door with an all-too familiar envelope in hand. Deck felt his heart rate soar as he beckoned her into his office.

Esme handed him the letter and stood before his desk, bracing herself for the harsh treatment she knew Deck usually delivered. Deck glanced through the resignation letter and quickly noted all the standard phrasing, and the familiar lack of an explanation about why she was unhappy. Deck thought back to when he'd first hired her, six months ago. She'd mentioned a tight-knit group of friends and a passion for the guitar.

"Of course, if you need to leave, you're free to do so," Deck began. "But, Esme, if you could sit down and tell me what prompted this decision, I would be very grateful."

Esme kept standing for a moment, totally thrown by Deck's gesture, and then she sat down and began to respond. "I don't think it was any one thing..."

Deck knew that she was just being polite and couldn't keep himself from interrupting. "Would it have anything to do with the time I screamed at you and called you a barely hominoid gargoyle?"

Esme blushed bright red.

"I shouldn't have done that. I know that I already push you and your teammates to the limit. There was no need to be cruel. I apologize for that."

"Thank you," Esme said, startled and wary. "I appreciate the apology."

"Is there any way I can convince you to stay?"

She shook her head. "I accepted a position elsewhere. I start in two weeks."

Deck nodded, dejected, as Esme stood. "But I do appreciate the apology," she repeated, her face an odd mix of apprehension and confusion. "Thank you."

"Wait...please." Deck asked her to sit down again. He took a breath. "Obviously, I don't have anything prepared as I wasn't expecting you to resign, but I want to thank you for your hard work and acknowledge some of the things that I have seen you do really well."

Deck then proceeded to walk through each of her projects and point out aspects of the work that she had achieved particularly well. He was good at details, so he took care to detail the points of her performance that had impressed him. At the end of his soliloquy, he paused, checking in with himself to see how he was doing. While part of him was uncomfortable over giving too much away and being overly generous, he felt good for simply telling the truth. He felt like she had earned the praise, even if she was leaving him.

Eventually, Deck realized Esme was staring at him, stunned. A long, strange moment stretched between them. Finally, she thanked him, almost more of a question than anything else. As she left, she lingered a moment at the door and thanked him again, this time with more certainty in her voice. And then she was gone.

Deck felt exhausted, both from processing the Clarity Compass within the conversation and from extending himself so drastically beyond the limits he was used to. But he also felt proud and hopeful for the first time in a long time.

As Esme's Volkswagen Westphalia pulled out of the parking lot, Deck took mental stock of his remaining employees. Which of them had felt the brunt of his disapproval most recently? Which seemed to have gone quiet? And which were still new enough that he might save the relationships? It came to him that rather than waiting for people to quit, he needed to proactively schedule one-on-one meetings with the each of his employees. He smiled wryly, as he knew word would get around quickly of his new and odd (for him) behavior once he started to have the conversations. He looked out his office door at his employees and realized, "These are my *crucial people*."

MATILDA

Matilda spent a good amount of time circumnavigating her Clarity Compass. She had not completed a full one hundred eighty turnaround on how she felt about Ling, but she realized that there were ways in which Ling was trying to be helpful based on his own Reality Map. She had also become uncomfortably aware of how her own behaviors and lack of performance had affected his opinion of her.

She was ready for the moment of truth.

Matilda rapped a knuckle on Ling's open door and leaned in from the doorframe. "Can we talk?"

Ling looked up from his screen. "Of course. Sit down."

As Matilda took a chair, she could feel her palms begin to moisten. "Thanks."

"How can I help?" Matilda could sense Ling's curiosity and concern. She rarely came to his office and she was obviously tenser than usual.

"Ling, I know you've been telling me for a while to be more strategic and to follow up more responsibly and responsively on assignments you've given me. In looking through many of my proposals, I've realized that you're right. I haven't been as strategic as I needed to be. I realized that I was viewing many of the projects you gave me as busywork instead of a chance to prove myself or contribute to the firm. I wanted to apologize to you for these errors in judgment. I want you to know that I'm going to be working on this and that I hope it will help me become senior partner. I also hope that you might be willing to give me some feedback on the game plan I'm creating to change these behaviors."

Ling gave a brief sigh and ran his fingers through his hair. "Look at it through my perspective, Matilda. I've got an employee clamoring for senior partnership who can't even complete the projects I've already given her. Does she deserve to be named senior partner?"

Matilda kept her cool. He was focusing on the one sentence about becoming senior partner rather than her apology. In retrospect, it would probably have been better to leave the "senior partner" material out. It also flashed in her mind that in all her preparation, she didn't even think of rescheduling the meeting as she had done with her friend. She probably avoided that so she didn't have to worry about it ahead of time, but could instead spontaneously drop by. This was probably not a good move in retrospect, but Matilda refocused and persevered, guided by the confidence and perspectives the Clarity Compasses of Self and Other had provided.

"Ling, I understand that you may feel I haven't lived up to your expectations, but I'm here now asking for further clarity and to learn directly from you. Are you willing to have that conversation?"

Ling gave her a calm, steady look, and she felt for one fleeting, terrifying moment that he could actually see into her soul. Thankfully, the moment passed. "I've got an hour free tomorrow at ten o'clock. Will that work for you?"

At ten o'clock the next day they met. They discussed Matilda's plan for becoming more strategic. At the end of reviewing her game plan, Ling said, "I'm glad to see that you prepared for this meeting and that you have a plan that if you follow will likely improve your strategic contribution to the firm."

Matilda replied, "I can understand your skepticism given how frequently you've mentioned this to me."

"And, Matilda, I'm looking forward to seeing you following up on assignments more closely."

Ling is relentless, Matilda thought. *How much do I have to extend myself to him?* She realized that he had at least acknowledged her on her game plan for being more strategic, which was a stretch for him. And even in the moment, she could appreciate that if she were him, she wouldn't get excited until she saw the promised results from a direct report of hers as well.

Nine months later, she was summarily called into Ling's office. He slid a piece of paper across the desk. He turned to his screen to work on his next email. As she read, she realized that Ling would've had to push this through for her, but he was acting as if it was nothing. She endearingly thought *Ling is still the same old Ling, but now he is also the Ling that has helped me reach senior partner.*

Creative Conversation Case Study Wrap Up: A Clarity Compass inspired Creative Conversation isn't going to resolve every issue, but Deck's brief interaction with Esme revealed a shift in him—he was working to be more respectful and appreciative of people. And while he wasn't able to convince Esme to stay, he was inspired to change his behavior towards his employees in a timely manner in order to prevent others from leaving. More importantly, Deck shifted his Reality Maps regarding his people, their value, and what they needed. Over time, he significantly altered his relationships with his employees.

In Matilda's case, in spite of her careful Creative Conversation planning, the conversation didn't go exactly as planned. There is no way to perfectly predict the Other's responses. But Matilda, with the Clarity Compass supporting her, persevered. Shifting her interactions and relationship with Ling required a number of subsequent Creative Conversations, and each created a bit more possibility. This gradual shifting in interactions and relationships is to be expected—especially with topics and situations that are extremely important or complex for both parties. It is hard to have a completely smooth and highly successful initial Creative Conversation.

CONCLUSION

The Challenges and Opportunities Ahead

L ike the fish having a difficult time being aware of the water it's swimming in, we are so immersed in our Reality Maps that we barely realize we are existing and acting within them. If we could somehow plug in our brains with someone else's, we could experience reality from a different perspective and experience directly just how subjective and particular our own reality is.

This subjectivity and lack of self-awareness is compounded by the fact that our Ego is deeply invested in confirmation bias, validating its own assumptions, and creating a kind of lockdown on our current reality. At the unconscious levels, the Ego works diligently to keep our lives feeling stable, predictable, and even comfortable. It seeks to control our external environment, but exerts even more control internally. Our Ego wants us to be right all the time—in particular situations and in life in general.

The Ego's insistence on being right is fine when our Reality Maps match reality perfectly, but given the complexity of the world, these instances tend to be rare. The Ego's confirmation bias inadvertently defends and maintains our Blind Spots. Consequently, life becomes filled with more conflict, difficulty, and struggle than if our Reality Maps were more accurate. For most people, it has become more and more difficult to discern the difference between their perceptions of the world and the world as it is—but for people who use the Clarity Compass, the chances of aligning their world view more closely with reality is far greater.

Our Biggest Hope

Our biggest hope for seeing beyond our Blind Spots and expanding our Reality Maps is to step into a Heart-oriented capacity for courage, to hold ambiguity, and to imagine new possibilities. As you begin this journey, the Ego will at first be resistant; but as you start to regularly use the Clarity Compass as an analytical tool for systematically opening up new understandings, your Ego will begin to slowly ease into new ways of thinking and being. This is true for specific situations and for the bigger picture.

The Clarity Compass creates a structure for our Egos to more easily invite and assimilate new understandings into our Reality Maps in a way that becomes less and less threatening. You will begin to see yourself transforming poor situations into good situations and good situations into great situations. More importantly, you will begin to transform your entire life. As you do so, you'll start to see where your old Reality Maps kept you stuck in patterns that your Ego had justified over and over again. Your Ego will open to allow more and more influence from your Heart, and you will find yourself having more freshness and aliveness in your life.

A Never-Ending Journey

My hope is that you've enjoyed reading this book, but more importantly, that it will make a difference for you and the people in your life.

Most of my clients, including Deck and Matilda, say that they reach a point where the energy they put into practicing the Clarity Compass becomes so natural that it's simply part of the way they function. As they practice using the Clarity Compass, they integrate it into their daily thinking and behavior, making them much more effective in multiple facets of their lives. At the same time, the Clarity Compass is not meant to be something you simply "get" and move on from. It's a never-ending inquiry that I myself am constantly learning more about and becoming more proficient at. Similarly, even as I have watched my clients become highly competent in naturally and spontaneously using the Clarity Compass and its related concepts, I note that as they continue to practice, they continue to reach even higher levels of mastery. I'm thrilled to watch them grow in the following ways:

1. **Problem solving**: By exposing the biases and Blind Spots of our Reality Maps, we become better at resolving personal and business challenges.
2. **Interpersonal skills:** By practicing the model and applying it to my Self and then the Other, communications and relational skills significantly improve.
3. **Leadership:** Because so much of the Clarity Compass model is about effectively creating outcomes with and for others, people begin to seek us out for greater leadership roles.

4. **Emotional intelligence:** We develop greater awareness, self-discipline, clarity of thinking, and compassion for Self and the Other that wins us greater mastery of the situations that challenge us in our personal and professional relationships. More importantly, we become more grounded in ourselves with more peace and wellbeing. This is a tremendous benefit for ourselves, but in turn it enables us to more powerfully impact the world around us in a positive way.

There are so many factors that determine our perspective, and our perspective influences the way we build relationships and pursue our goals. Gandhi said, "Happiness is when what you think, what you say, and what you do are in harmony." Regularly attending to the questions and challenges the Clarity Compass presents can help you reach that alignment.

I've seen people transformed by the smallest incremental turns toward greater self-knowledge. By using the Clarity Compass to orient yourself within yourself, toward others, and toward the world, over time, not only will you become better at moving challenging situations forward, your Reality Maps will shift and you will attract more harmonious, meaningful, and powerful relationships on personal and professional levels. The Clarity Compass process brings about greater wellbeing, relationships, and community, as well as effectiveness and love.

ABOUT THE AUTHOR

Dr. Brit Poulson is the owner and principal of Clarity Compass Consulting, www.clarity-compass.com, a leadership consulting firm specializing in transformative executive coaching and leadership development programs. Brit has been integrating the fields of management consulting, business psychology, and leadership coaching since 1983. Brit earned a Ph.D. in psychodynamic and group psychology at the Pacifica Graduate Institute. He also has an M.A. in human growth and potential from the University of West Georgia and a B.A. in accounting and Business Administration from Troy State University.

CPSIA information can be obtained
at www.ICGtesting.com
Printed in the USA
BVHW04s1122250518
517263BV00001B/116/P